BREAKING THE WORRY HABIT . . . FOREVER!

This book belongs to

_____

*a woman who
trusts God.*

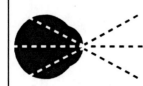

This Large Print Book carries the
Seal of Approval of N.A.V.H.

BREAKING THE WORRY HABIT . . . FOREVER!

ELIZABETH GEORGE

THORNDIKE PRESS

A part of Gale, Cengage Learning

Detroit • New York • San Francisco • New Haven, Conn • Waterville, Maine • London

GALE
CENGAGE Learning

LIBRARY OF CONGRESS CATALOGING-IN-PUBLICATION DATA

George, Elizabeth, 1944–
    Breaking the worry habit — forever! / by Elizabeth George. — Large print ed.
      p. cm.
    "Christian Large Print originals."
    ISBN-13: 978-1-59415-302-0 (softcover : alk. paper)
    ISBN-10: 1-59415-302-7 (softcover : alk. paper)
    1. Worry — Religious aspects — Christianity. 2. Christian women — Religious life. 3. Large type books. I. Title.
BV4908.5.G47 2010
248.8′43—dc22
                           2009026771

Published in 2009 by arrangement with Harvest House Publishers.

Printed in the United States of America

2 3 4 5 6   14 13 12 11 10

ED110

ACKNOWLEDGMENTS

CONTENTS

AN INVITATION TO WIN OVER WORRY . . . ONCE AND FOR ALL

If you're holding this book in your hand, I'm sure there's a good reason — you're tired of paying the price for your habit of worrying. You know it's harmful. You know it's useless. And you know it doesn't change a thing. Instead, it's destroying your health, relationships, and peace of mind.

Well, good news! You are not alone. Worry affects everyone. In fact, for decades worry was my constant companion. After I realized worry denies the power of God and produces no positive results, I knew it had to go. Because my own methods of getting rid of anxiety weren't making any difference, I turned to the Bible for help. That's when — and where — I found God's life-changing truths that showed me the way to break my habit of worrying. I invite you to join me, a recovering worrier, as I share what I discovered that works. And because it comes from God's Word, it can work for you too.

Breaking the Worry Habit . . . Forever! looks at 12 areas of daily life that cause anxiety in a woman's heart. For example, have you ever had a health problem, or a child who struggled, or aging, sick, or dying parents? How do you handle money problems, fear, your life circumstances, and guilt? Does making a tough decision send you into a fresh worry fit? And then there's wondering about what people think of you! Take heart. There's no need to worry about anything . . . ever again. By the grace of God and with His help, you can eliminate worry altogether . . . and forever.

1
What's Wrong with Me?

And who of you by being worried
can add a single hour to his life?
MATTHEW 6:27 NASB

There are certain red-letter days in every woman's life. The memory of one of mine — and recalling the anxiety that arrived with it — will never go away. It all began with a routine annual well-woman exam. The first alarm that went off was the look of concern on my doctor's face. The second sounded when she said, "I don't like the look of things. I'm going to order a biopsy." Then came an even louder alarm. The biopsy results contained one very frightening word — "abnormal."

I stared at the floor, not wanting to hear what my doctor was saying but hearing it nevertheless. "We can't be certain whether it's cancerous or not until we take a further look. But things are definitely not normal. I'm ordering a surgery to remove the growth."

In the end, my abnormal cell formation was not cancer. For that I am deeply grateful! But, believe me, that was one time in my life when I went through a serious bout with worry, fear, anxiety, and speculation.

Health issues are fertile soil for the all-too-easily-cultivated habit of worry. I know, and I speak from experience. My real call to battle was not for war in the *physical* realm. No, it was for war in the *spiritual* realm! I went into a full-throttled tailspin spiritually. It was as though I dropped to ground zero in my faith and trust in God. After a time of total, out-of-control failure, I realized I had to get my act together. I had to stop moving in the destructive direction I was letting my mind and emotions take me. I had to halt, regroup, retrain, and move out in an entirely different direction — a better direction, the right direction. I had to chisel away on my worry habit so I could live with the peace that only God can provide when we trust in Him with all our heart.

THE VAST SCOPE OF WORRIES

Once something is wrong — or even *might* be wrong — with us, our minds run wild! We can start worrying backward about what triggered a health crisis and rapidly work our way forward through every possible scenario and development . . . right up to the sound of dirt being dropped on our casket in a grave! Nothing and no one is spared from being included in our vast scope of worries.

"What about the kids? What will their lives be like if I die or am disabled? And my husband? What in the world will he do without my help? Why, he can hardly find a pair of matching socks! And my parents? Oh, dear! They have enough health issues and worries of their own. It's not natural for a child to precede parents in death!"

On and on . . . and on! . . . the anxieties cascade. And so does the adrenaline . . . and the stomach acid. And up and up . . . and up! . . . go our heart rate and our blood pressure. At times we're so distraught we can't eat a bite. And then there are those days when we eat nonstop, hoping that we will find some "comfort food" in the mass ingested. Maybe we even consider — or ask our doctor for — some kind of medication to help us cope with our overwhelming anxiety, to calm us down, to at least allow us to get a good night's sleep. Each night brings no rest, and each day's sunrise offers no hope or relief. It seems we may as well be dead.

God's Take on Health, Life, and Death

Have you ever heard the axiom, "The moment you are born, you begin to die"? Or the one that says, "The two things you cannot avoid in life are death and taxes"? Life and health are both gifts from God and should never be taken for granted. But it's also true that both are fleeting. Moses addressed death and put life into its transitory perspective when he wrote:

The days of our lives are seventy years; and if by reason of strength they are eighty years, yet their boast is only labor and sorrow; for it is soon cut off, and we fly away (Psalm 90:10).

So, as you can see, you can't avoid death. And as Jesus implied in His query in Matthew 6:27 — "Who of you by being worried can add a single hour to his life?" — you cannot add to the length of your life. There-fore, as Jesus is suggesting, why should you worry about the reality and timing of your death?

But health and life still need to be under-stood from a proper biblical perspective. Consider these truths drawn from God's Word.

Good health is natural and normal. What a great and gracious God we have! He al-lows the rain to fall on the just and the un-just (Matthew 5:45). The vast majority of people on earth enjoy relatively good health for most of their lives. Oh, there's the occa-sional flu bug, bad cold, or strained muscle. But normally most people experience good health. Day after day, even year after year, we go merrily on our way without a thought about our health because there are no physi-cal issues or ailments. And that's the way it should be. Even in the midst of a sin-cursed world, God has engineered our bodies to feel good and function without pain when we are well. Mankind is allowed to enjoy His grace when it comes to physical health.

We are not guaranteed a life free of pain or illness. When sin entered the world, it brought pain, disease, illness, and death. As a human, you, along with every other person on earth, are under the curse that resulted from Adam and Eve's sin in the garden of Eden. Jesus wanted His followers and you and me to know the hard truth. Bluntly, He said, "In the world you will have tribulation" (John 16:33). Such tribulation can be in the form of religious persecution, strained personal relationships, or the relentless process of growing old! God never promised His children a life of health. Maybe this is why the apostle Paul never asked others to pray for his health. Nor did he ever pray for the *physical* health of his readers. What he did pray for was their *spiritual* health (Colossians 1:9–11).

> No matter what comes your way here on earth, no matter what pain or agony you face, set your worries aside and look heavenward!

When my husband pastored and taught a senior citizens' Sunday school class some years ago, he heard many of these dear people share one particular verse that comforted them after a spouse died. It was from a description of "the new heaven": "God will wipe away every tear from their eyes; there shall be no more death, nor sorrow, nor crying. There shall be no more pain, for the former things have passed away" (Revelation 21:4). This scripture describes the reality and angst of suffering in life . . . but also the welcomed delights and promised well-being that await God's people as they spend eternity in His presence. No matter what comes your way here on earth, no matter what pain or agony you face, set your worries aside and look heavenward!

Physical pain is not necessarily bad. It's great to enjoy health and a vibrant body, but you and I can be thankful our bodies also alert us when things are not right. Depending on the location and nature of the pain, a medical professional can usually help us. We may have to bear a short-lived illness or condition, but generally we are soon back on our feet and everything is back to normal. If the pain hadn't developed, we wouldn't have known something was wrong. I'm sure you've heard of or known someone who went to the doctor with an early problem or pain and was told that action at the sign of an early symptom actually saved their life. So the next time you have an ache or pain, first thank God for the warning. Then take action. Don't wait! Find out what's causing the pain and get it taken care of.

Physical pain is an opportunity to trust God. Sometimes our pain is caused by a condition that lasts for a longer period of time — weeks, months, years, or even a lifetime. What do we do when this happens? The typical first response is to ask, "Why, God? And why me? What have I done to deserve this?" But a better response is to pray, "God, what do You want to teach me?"

The apostle Paul had one of these painful, lingering conditions. He called it his "thorn in the flesh." Paul struggled with his thorn. In fact, he prayed God would take it away. And he prayed that same prayer three times (2 Corinthians 12:7–8)!

What was God's answer? He assured His servant Paul, "My grace is sufficient for you, for My strength is made perfect in weakness" (verse 9). The Lord showed Paul that even though he was suffering, he — Paul — was not alone. God was with him, strengthening him. Paul's pain and suffering remained, but the resource to deal with it was there as well. He just had to trust God to strengthen him as he suffered through pain that was not going to go away. At last Paul got it! He was able to declare:

Therefore most gladly I will rather boast in my infirmities, that the power of Christ

*may rest upon me. Therefore I take plea-
sure in infirmities, in reproaches, in needs,
in persecutions, in distresses, for Christ's
sake. For when I am weak, then I am strong*
(verses 9–10).

When we as Christians suffer, it's always an opportunity to trust God and give Him glory. And when we trust Him, we rest in Him . . . which brings us peace of mind and soul. As I'm sitting here at my computer experiencing (at least for today and for the moment) reasonably good health, it's easier for me to talk about trusting God during times of pain, illness, and physical decline than it would be if I were actually suffering physically. But I always pray that when that time comes — and it will! — I will follow Paul's example and trust in God's grace through the pain and suffering. And I pray the same prayer for you. When we as Christians suffer, it's always an opportunity to trust God and give Him glory.

When long-term suffering shows up on your doorstep, remember these words from American preacher Henry Ward Beecher: "Every tomorrow has two handles. We can take hold of it by the handle of anxiety, or by the handle of faith."[1] The choice is yours. Be sure you grab hard on the handle of faith!

Spiritual health is more important than physical health. I'm sure you value your good health as much as I do. But when you become a Christian, your physical life takes a backseat to your spiritual life. A Christian embraces and nurtures an eternal perspective. Your concerns — and mine — should take on a heavenly dimension. Again, Paul has help for us. He shows us the way we are to view life and health:

> *For our citizenship is in heaven, from which we also eagerly wait for the Savior, the Lord Jesus Christ, who will transform our lowly body that it may be conformed to His glorious body* (Philippians 3:20–21).

How many prayer times or meetings have you been in where most of the requests were for people's health? These prayers are important, but I remind you again that Paul never asked the readers of any of his letters to pray for his health while he was suffering or in prison. What were some of the things he asked others to pray for on his behalf?

   ✺ *A courageous heart.* Paul desired boldness in his preaching, a boldness only God could give (Ephesians 6:19).

❧ *An open door.* Paul needed an open door from God to preach the gospel (Colossians 4:3).

❧ *A clear message.* Paul wished for his preaching to clearly communicate the message of Christ so that many could hear and believe (Colossians 4:3).

And what were his prayers for his readers? Here are a few of many:

❧ *Wisdom and knowledge.* Paul wished that his readers would also be filled with God's wisdom and knowledge (Colossians 1:9).

❧ *A worthy walk.* Paul desired that Christ's followers would "walk worthy of the Lord" (Colossians 1:10).

❧ *Inner strength.* Paul wanted believers to be strengthened with power through God's Spirit in the inner man (Ephesians 3:16).

I'm sure you're getting the message. Your life and health are important. However, they're only temporary and earthly. But you, as a child of God, are moving toward a better

21

existence, one that is eternal and heavenly. You are merely a sojourner and a pilgrim passing through this life (1 Peter 2:11). But while you are here and on your way to glory, be a good steward of the body God has given you for His work here on earth. Take care of your health, but don't dwell on it too much. And by all means, don't worry about it! Instead be disciplined and do your part.

Doing Your Part

I've spent most of this chapter encouraging you not to be overly concerned about your physical health. But did you notice the key word — "overly"? To make sure you keep your worry about your own health (or that of family members or friends) in perspective and under control, here are a few things you can do in the form of a to-do list.

✓ *Watch over your body.* Even though you are a kingdom citizen, you still reside in a body, which has a stewardship attached to it. Your body is "the temple of the Holy Spirit" and "you are not your own" (1 Corinthians 6:19). Paul then added, "You were bought at a price; therefore glorify God in your body and in your spirit, which are God's" (1 Corinthians 6:19–20). Taking care of your body is one way you can glorify God.

✓ *Watch what you eat.* God wanted to protect His people so He prescribed a set of dietary laws for them. For example, the heathen nations in the Old Testament had no understanding of disease and the need to cook food before eating it. But the Israelites had God's instructions. Even though most Christians don't strictly follow the Old Testament dietary laws today, the principles behind them are wise ones: Watch what and how much you eat, and how it's prepared. Reading the back of any package or can of food will tell you if you should eat it or not! For several decades I've read books and articles regularly on diet and nutrition. Try it! It will keep you more aware and knowledgeable — and careful — about what you put into your mouth . . . which goes into a body that belongs to *God!*

✓ *Watch your weight.* This will probably take care of itself if you watch what you eat. But it also helps to weigh yourself every day. Select an "ideal" weight for your health, body structure, and lifestyle. Then strive to stay as close to that weight as possible. I track my weight daily on a graph. As the saying goes, one picture is worth a thousand words! I can see exactly what's going on (or up, or down)! Don't do what I did. For years I read and knew that I should watch what I eat and watch my weight, but I just didn't do it. Wow, what a difference these two practices make each day! Also remember that self-control is a fruit of the Spirit (Galatians 5:23). This makes your eating habits and your weight spiritual issues as well as physical ones.

✓ *Exercise regularly.* Doctors and nutritionists agree that regular exercise promotes good health. Paul told his protégée, young Timothy, that "bodily exercise profits a little" (1 Timothy 4:8). So plan some exercise into your life, even if it's only a little! Again, it's a matter of stewardship, of taking care of God's body. I have less than zero time to exercise. I have to weigh the benefit of each decision I make about the use of my time. But I do try to fit in at least a time to walk each day. I've learned to view exercise as an investment, not in the longevity of my life (that's up to God), but in the quality of my life (that's my contribution).

✓ *Have regular checkups.* Jim and I have a longtime friend who recently had his annual physical exam. The doctors found a problem and immediately removed a cancerous growth before it had time to spread. Regular doctor visits don't catch everything, but they are one way we can do our part to detect or prevent illnesses. You can sit at home and worry about the possibility of a problem . . . or you can have a checkup and know that everything seems to be okay. Action and information will check your habit of worrying about the unknown and have a calming effect on you.

> *You can sit at home and worry about the possibility of a problem . . . or you can get a checkup.*

✓ *Follow up on warning signs.* I said earlier that pain is a bodily mechanism that alerts us to a problem. Well, it seems some people would rather worry about their pain than go to the doctor to find out the cause. They're so afraid of what it might be that they put off a checkup until it's too late to find out and make a difference. When you have a pain, which could be something or nothing, don't worry about it. Do something. Go to the doctor and find out!

✓ *Keep your focus on heaven.* Warning: If you're not careful, you can become so attached to this world and your physical health that you lose sight of your heavenly calling. This doesn't mean you're not to care about physical things like your health. What it does mean is that you are to hold on to your physical well-being "lightly." Then, if and when ill health and even death arrive, they can be viewed as merely a transition. The apostle Paul had this upward, heavenly focus when he declared, "For to me, to live is Christ, and to die is gain." He also desired "to depart and be with Christ, which is far better" (Philippians 1:21–23). As the hymn teaches, "Turn your eyes upon Jesus, look full in His wonderful face, and the things of earth shall grow strangely dim, in the light of His glory and grace."[2]

✓ *Trust in the providence of God.* Do whatever is necessary to nurture this trust! It's vital to breaking any tendencies you have to worry about anything, including your health. Your consuming passion should always be for God's will — not your own. This means you should pray for and desire God's will above all things — including feeling good, being healthy, and living a long life. Pray as Jesus did: "Your will be done on earth as it is in heaven" (Matthew 6:10). Also make it a habit (. . . and this is a good one!) to read your Bible on a regular basis. This habit, like nothing else, will keep your mind focused on God. Then when things happen, your first thought will be, "Don't worry. Trust God instead." Because you've seen God in action in the pages of your Bible, you'll know about His nature, strength, and power. And that translates into a growing trust in Him.

Breaking the Worry Habit . . . Forever!

I'm a person who used to sleep with my pillow under my stomach to comfort my bleeding ulcer instead of sleeping with the pillow under my head. Finally I acknowledged that worry is a terrible sin . . . and a terrible habit. As I read my Bible and grew as a Christian, I couldn't help but notice there are so *many* commands in the Bible telling God's followers not to worry! I grabbed onto these two and began to pull them out when I felt my stomach burning or caught myself wondering and worrying. Jesus commanded: "Do not worry about your life" (Matthew 6:25). And Paul commanded: "Be anxious for nothing" (Philippians 4:6).

The truth is, worrying goes against God's will for your life. Worrying also affects your health. Medical studies have affirmed this observation by Dr. Charles Mayo, cofounder of the internationally renowned Mayo Clinic:

Worry affects circulation, the heart, the glands, the whole nervous system. I have never known a man who died from overwork, but many who died from doubt.[3]

I hope you're agreeing that worrying is a bad habit. It offends God. And it damages your life and health. A habit is anything you do on a regular basis. Habits can be good ones . . . or bad ones. Reading your Bible and praying are good habits that you want to be a part of your life. But any habit, whether it's an action or attitude or thought process that tempts you to turn your heart away from God and onto yourself is a bad one and must be changed and dealt with dramatically and drastically.

Worry is definitely one of the actions that takes your eyes off God. Worry says that "this" (whatever "this" is that you're worrying about) is something that can't be handled by God, with God, or by His grace. This attitude is the exact opposite of trusting God. You might as well be wearing a T-shirt or pin that says, "I don't trust God." The goal of spiritual growth is to exchange the bad habit of worrying with the excellent habit of trusting God. Whatever your situation, do your part. Do all you can. But most of all, be sure you turn your concern over to God!

Trust in the LORD with all your heart.
PROVERBS 3:5

Blessed are all those who put their trust in Him.
PSALM 2:12

2
MORE MONTH THAN MONEY

I have learned in whatever state I am,
to be content: I know how to be abased,
and I know how to abound.

PHILIPPIANS 4:11-12

The weather had finally cleared. It had been an awful winter! Storm after storm had dumped a record amount of snow on the friendly suburb near Detroit where Sue Higgins lived. But on this day the weather had turned warm and sunny. You would think the bright, cheery day would have raised Sue's spirits, but not so. The black cloud of worry that shadowed Sue's life wasn't about to go away.

The last few years had been a financial roller coaster for the Higgins family. Bill, Sue's husband of 15 years, was in middle management at the main office of a major automobile plant. There had been some previous scares, but Bill had managed to hang on to his position. Bill and Sue had talked about the rumored cutbacks and layoffs, but yesterday the company had formally announced a cutback of 8000 jobs at the plant. To make matters worse, she and Bill had never quite gotten around to trimming their budget. Looking back, Sue wished the family hadn't taken that trip to Disney World last August. They were *still* trying to pay off the credit card debt that had mounted up during their vacation. And that wasn't the only bill they were behind on!

Sue paced and wrung her hands as she tried not to look at the new pile of overdue notices that had arrived in today's mail and lay on the kitchen table. Again and again she groaned, "What are we going to do? These job cuts usually begin near the top, with management. We're behind in all our payments. Christmas is coming. Both of the kids need braces. If we don't get the car fixed soon, we'll need a new one. And we committed ourselves to housing a missionary family while they're here on their furlough. Oh, wow! That'll cost! Where is the money for daily life going to come from?" Sue's financial situation seemed so hopeless.

FACING A FEW FACTS ABOUT FINANCES

When I was growing up, I often heard a saying that's stuck with me: "If the shoe fits, wear it." As I sense the heart-pounding fear Sue is experiencing as she suffers and worries in the area of finances, I'm tempted to wear that shoe . . . again. Her story strikes home in far too many places. I've had my own bouts with killer trials in the financial realm. I remember all too well . . .

- ✸ Being a newlywed while Jim and I were still in college without our parents' monetary support.

- ✸ Moving as a couple from Tennessee to Los Angeles, California, where the cost of living was a whopping four times more.

- ✸ Quitting my job when Baby #1 arrived.

- ✸ Living as a family of four on a severely

32

reduced income when my husband quit his job to go to seminary and train for ministry.

✎ Doing all I could to hold down expenses at home when our two daughters were in college at the same time for four years.

I still wake up in the night with my stomach churning and my mind running wild, tempted to wonder and worry about not only the present but the future.

So, you see, Sue is not alone in her fears and concerns! And others are in the same boat. According to the well-known Penn State Worry Questionnaire, when asked, "During the past four weeks, have you been bothered by feeling worried, tense or anxious most of the time?" ninety percent of those questioned answered *yes.*

And financial worries are right at the top of the list of things that cause us to feel worried, tense, or anxious. Just last week while being interviewed on a nationwide call-in radio program, I couldn't help but notice every single caller was concerned with her personal economic condition. My interview was on the many Bible promises presented in my book *Following God with All*

Your Heart, yet somehow finances worked its way into all of the questions. Callers' fears were my cue to zero in on the chapters on contentment from my book. After the program was done, I thought about the common denominator of their questions — fear about finances. It made sense. Each person who phoned in wanted desperately to follow God with all her heart . . . but each was also wrestling with money matters.

Recently I looked through a newspaper that showed a visual graphic of a health scale with the headline "Money weighs us down." The survey taken was meant to show how many people had made weight loss their focus for the new year. However, the dial showed that seventy percent of those polled admitted they were worried about finances while only thirty percent were worried about their weight and health.[1]

And today, when I turned on my computer to continue writing this book about worry, the headline on my home page heralded, "Consumer confidence hits new low." And because (I confess) I'm always tempted to worry about finances, I read further:

Americans' mood about the economy darkened further in January, sending a widely watched barometer of consumer sentiment to a new low, a private research group said Tuesday, as people worry about their jobs and watch their retirement funds dwindle . . . [The] director of The Conference Board Consumer Research Center said in a statement, "Looking ahead, consumers remain quite pessimistic about the state of the economy and about their earnings."[2]

Since Adam and Eve were forced out of the garden of Eden (Genesis 3), mankind has faced the problem of finding and providing food, clothing, and shelter on a daily basis. Provision is a basic, practical area of life and existence. And it's a common — and daily — cause for worry. To have food takes money. To have clothes involves money. And to have shelter requires money. For most people, money comes from having a job, whether that job is done in a place of business, through a profession, on a farm, or in a home office.

But Jesus instructs us clearly regarding worry about these basic elements of life. He told His followers, *"Do not worry about your life, what you will eat or what you will drink: nor about your body, what you will put on"* (Matthew 6:25).

"Do Not Worry"

As you think about Matthew 6:25, you can't help but acknowledge that our Lord has a command — not advice, not a financial tip, not a suggestion, not something for us to think about, but a command — for us when it comes to worrying about the basics of life. Note the force of Jesus' words as He states simply and plainly:

"*Do not* worry about your life" (NKJV).

"*Stop* worrying about your life" (Williams).

"*Do not* be anxious about your life here" (TCNT).

"*Put away* anxious thoughts about [your life]" (NEB).

Jesus' message is crystal clear. It can't be missed or misinterpreted. It's to the point and is delivered in three simple, understandable words: *Do not worry.* His followers were worrying — anxious and overly concerned — about the basics of daily living. They were fretting about food and clothes — so much so that they were losing their focus on God, on one hundred percent devotion to

Him and living out His kingdom priorities. Their service to God (which is eternal) was diluted and at risk due to their obsession with daily basics (which are temporal and earthly).

It's a fact that fear and worry immobilize us in our kingdom work. They distract us from our worship and love of God. And our service to God and His people is hampered and blocked when we worry about ourselves and fail to trust Him.

COUNTING ON GOD

Why should we worry about food when God is fully able to — and will — provide for His own? He can even prepare food for us in the desert — even set a table and fill it in the presence of our enemies (Psalm 23:5). As with Elijah, God can choose to use a raven to feed us (1 Kings 17:4–6). As with a widow and her son in yet another dire situation, God can cause us to eat for many days *after* we give up our last handful of food (1 Kings 17:10-16).

As you read the entire message from Jesus in Matthew 6:25–34, you'll discover at least six reasons not to worry . . . which are six reasons why you can trust God and count on His provision for you and His oversight of every detail of your life.

1. You are valuable to God (verse 26).
2. Your situation is under God's control, not yours (verse 27).
3. You will be taken care of (verses 28–30).
4. Your needs are known to God (verses 31–32).
5. Your pursuits should focus on God (verse 33).
6. Your life should be lived one day at a time (verse 34).

Doing Your Part

When life gets tough, you and I have at least one serious spiritual choice *we* get to make. We get to choose whether to obsess and fixate on something earthly like our financial status or whether to look up and count on God's forever promises. When we opt for the upward gaze — the God gaze — then we can, with a clear head and undivided heart, proceed to do the important work God has called us to, His kingdom work here on earth.

And there's another decision we get to make on a more practical level. We get to decide whether to use our time and energy worrying or whether to spend it doing something about the situation, the problem. What can we do when money is tight, scarce, or nonexistent? Here are a handful of things we can do, a few key ways we can put our time, anxiety, and fears to work in a positive way.

✓ First and foremost, *keep your head and your heart in God's Word.* Amazingly, reading the Bible has a calming effect. Between the pages of your Bible, you'll find encouragement while you suffer, instruction about how to endure, promises to cling to and trust, truths about God's love and provision for His own, and facts about His total ability to take care of His people. During hard times, be sure you cultivate the soil where worry tends to germinate — your heart! It was Jesus who told us, "Let not your heart be troubled, neither let it be afraid" (John 14:27). Doses of God's Word will help you stay confident and hopeful when the road looks impossible.

✓ Next, *get help.* Look around. Do you know someone who's making it through life on less, little, or nothing? Ask them for pointers . . . and take notes! What are they doing about their problem, and what are they doing about their attitude? Find out who in your church or community gives financial advice to others. I know a couple who met regularly with a financial consultant who guided them in overcoming massive credit card debts. It took three years, but they did it. What a victory! Don't be ashamed or afraid to ask for help. Other options are checking out budgeting books from the public library or taking a class at the community center on managing your money.

> *Replace worry with prayer. How do you do that? You make the decision to pray whenever you catch yourself worrying.*

✓ You can never do too much of this next remedy for worry and financial pressures: *Pray!* When you pray, you're following God's pattern for a quiet heart. Philippians 4:6–7 commands us to "be anxious for nothing." These verses go on to give the solution to all worry: "In everything by prayer and supplication, with thanksgiving, let your requests be made known to God." The result? "The peace of God, which surpasses all understanding will guard your hearts and minds through Christ Jesus."

These verses use four terms for prayer ("prayer," "supplication," "thanksgiving," and "requests") to send one message: Replace worry with prayer. This section of each chapter of this book is called *Doing Your Part*. Replacing worry with prayer will require you to do something — to make a decision to pray when you catch yourself worrying. So begin now to do your part. Starting today — this minute — pray as soon as you feel the first tinge of fear, worry, and anxiety in your heart. Through prayer, cast your cares — financial and every other kind — on the Lord (1 Peter 5:7). And don't forget to ask God for wisdom concerning your finances (James 1:5). Don't miss out on the peace God guarantees to those who pray.

✓ Here's another thing you can do: *Work hard.* The Bible speaks to us about our role in our personal provision and the provision of our loved ones. The apostle Paul stated, "If anyone will not work, neither shall he eat" (2 Thessalonians 3:10). Paul pointed to his own behavior, reminding his readers that he, Timothy, and Silas "were not disorderly among you; nor did we eat anyone's bread free of charge, but worked with labor and toil night and day" (verse 7).

So, if you work at a job, work hard — harder than anyone else, for you serve the Lord Christ, not man (Colossians 3:24). When it comes to layoffs, employers are less likely to lay off a good, solid, dependable, productive, hard worker. If you work at home, work hard — harder than you think you have to. If you don't have an income-producing job, work hard! See how much work you can personally do without paying someone else to do it. See how hard you can cook so your family doesn't have to eat out. See how hard you can work at saving money in as many ways as possible. The model woman in Proverbs 31 worked hard managing her household and refused to be idle (verse 27).

✓ Even the sound of this one hurts, but it

works: *Cut back.* It's alarming how easy it is to be excessive or to amass things or subscribe to services we don't need. In our latest round of cutting back, Jim and I opted to cancel our television cable service. We also canceled a phone line and now use our cell phones exclusively. What can you cut back? Do you have a lawnmower *and* a lawn service? Mow the lawn yourself! That's what I did in one of our cash crunches when our daughters were in college. Do you have some clutter you can cut back and sell in a yard or tag sale? Our family has done this on an annual basis. Do you get out in the car every day just to get out? Could you cut back to every other day . . . or twice a week? When gas hit $4 a gallon, I trimmed my trips to once a week. Opportunities to cut back are everywhere . . . if you're looking for them. Fine-tune your money-excess awareness.

✓ Got kids? *Talk with your children* (or family). It's easy to raise children who want everything and think they can and should have it. But it's also easy to cultivate diligence and responsibility in kids. I recently read an article that advised parents to sit down and talk candidly with their children about the state of their family finances. Let them know there's a shortage of funds, and tell them why — the economy, cutbacks, layoffs, the high price of gasoline, and the like. The parents featured in the article did this and were delightfully surprised to see their kids listen soberly, willingly agree to do their part, and eagerly take on their areas of responsibility with a maturity they hadn't witnessed in them before. They liked being treated as important parts of the family's financial solution. (And they loved telling their parents to be sure and turn out the lights!) One wonderful thing about a family is that it always boils down to "one for all and all for one."

✓ Never forget you can do your part . . . in spite of others. I receive a lot of mail from wives who are trying to watch out and cut back in the area of spending but whose husbands aren't. There isn't much wives in this situation can do. But we can share (not scream!) our concerns, pray, and do our part. So if you're married, *you* be a careful manager of money, no matter what. It's a godly character trait God wants you to possess. Let pleasing God and growing in thrift and diligence be your reward. And besides, every little bit *you* do and save helps!

TAPPING INTO GOD'S PEACE

I admit (again!) that I have all the tendencies of a full-fledged worrywart . . . especially in the area of everyday finances. In the past, peace has eluded me as I lived with eczema up to my elbows . . . and a bleeding ulcer . . . and colitis. Believe me, I've had to consciously learn how to break my own worry habit. And, as you well know, life never fails to present temptations for worrying. But several rich, instructive verses have come to my rescue and shown me the way to overcome my natural inclination to worry, not only about money matters but about everything! They point us to the path of personal and lasting peace of mind. Read them now and let them wash over you.

Not that I speak in regard to need, for I have learned in whatever state I am, to be content: I know how to be abased, and I know how to abound. Everywhere and in all things I have learned both to be full and to be hungry, both to abound and to suffer need. I can do all things through Christ who strengthens me (Philippians 4:11–13).

As I've memorized, studied, and tried to live these verses, I've learned several keys to tapping into God's peace whenever I have a need. First, realize *there is no need to worry about need.* Why? Because "the LORD is my shepherd; I shall not want" (Psalm 23:1). Therefore, there is never any need to fear being without what we truly need. There is never anything to complain about. There is never any reason to be under any pressure of want.

> *When you encounter a difficulty, a challenge, or a speed bump on your path, remember, you "can do all things through Christ who strengthens [you]."*

Next, understand *we can learn to be content.* I love this concept! Whew! It means I can be content. There's hope! Contentment — or "soul-sufficiency"[3] — is learned! It's not a part of my position in Christ, it's not a fruit of the Spirit, and it doesn't arrive with salvation. We are not born with it, nor does it just mystically appear. No, it is learned.

How is contentment learned? *Salvation, circumstances, and trials teach us contentment.* Paul (the writer of these verses) points to some of the elements that initiated him into contentment — elements of joy and sorrow, plenty and want. He had tasted hunger, thirst, fasting, cold, nakedness, physical suffering, mental torture, persecution . . . and more! And he had experienced prosperity and plenty. We could say that life is made up of many "states," many conditions, pressures, and experiences — both bad and good.

However, *the strength of Christ enables us to do what must be done.* In other words, whatever we need to do, we can do! Why? Because we are in Christ. And Christ's grace is sufficient. And His power rests on us (2 Corinthians 12:9). Christ infuses His strength into us. He is our wonderful helper, and He's always standing by us. He never fails to supply us with all we need or require to endure, to go on, to handle whatever life brings our way.

When my husband traveled to Australia for ministry, he learned a saying from "down under." The Aussies love to say, "No worries!" These two words express a principle we learn from Philippians 4:11–13. Whatever happens, whatever we face, whatever state we're in, whatever we lack, we have "no worries!" Why? Because we can do all things through Christ who strengthens us. Make it your goal for the rest of today to recall — even out loud — this truth and promise from God to you when you encounter a difficulty, a challenge, or a speed bump on your path. Then do it again tomorrow . . . and every day. This is how you tap into God's peace and cultivate contentment.

Breaking the Worry Habit . . . Forever!

Is the desire of your heart to break the unnerving practice of worrying? Do you wish for peace of mind, regardless of the flurry of your days and the rush of temptations to give in to worry? Do you want the maturity and rocklike character that comes with pressing on right through your problems with a heart at rest and the strength of Christ? If so, enjoying peace every minute boils down to determining to obey Jesus' command: "Do not worry." Do not be anxious! Don't give in to worry! You will have to stop being anxious!

I know this sounds hard, maybe even impossible, but this is what Jesus says you must do. In the Greek language, Jesus' command,

"Do not worry" or "Do not be anxious," includes the idea of stopping what is already being done. In other words, we are to stop worrying . . . *and* never start it again. The various translations I shared earlier in this chapter describe the rigidity and determination we must have to overcome fear, worry, and anxiety. They use some very active, cut-and-dried, harsh words when it comes to worrying: "Do not" worry. "Stop" worrying. "Put away" worry.

On the heels of this negative — *Do not worry* — comes a powerful positive action: *Trust in the Lord.* As one Bible commentary points out:

> Worry presents us with the dual temptation to distrust God and to substitute fear for practical action. Worry means paying attention to what we cannot change instead of putting our energies to work in effective ways. Jesus made it clear that worry takes away from life rather than adding anything to it. We can counteract worry by doing what we can and trusting where we can't. When we work for God and wait on his timing, we won't have time to worry. When we seek first to honor God as king and conform our lives to his righteousness, worry will always find us otherwise occupied.[4]

What a blessing it is when you're preoccupied with the Lord! You won't have time to fret and stew. You'll truly be living in the land of "no worries!"

Blessed is the man who trusts in the LORD
and whose trust is the LORD.
For he will be like a tree planted by the water,
that extends its roots by a stream
and will not fear when the heat comes;
but its leaves will be green,
and it will not be anxious in a year of drought
nor cease to yield fruit.
JEREMIAH 17:7–8 NASB

3
'TIL DEATH DO US PART

Therefore a man shall leave his father and mother and be joined to his wife, and they shall become one flesh.

GENESIS 2:24

Hospital waiting rooms are about the worst places on earth for sitting and waiting! Gladys concluded this as she panned the waiting room where she currently found herself. Like her, everyone else was in a daze. It seemed every single person there had sagging shoulders and furrowed foreheads. Deep concern — and fear! — was evident and written all over their faces. What were they "waiting" on? Some waited for the person they had brought in for a cancer treatment to reappear through the swinging doors. Others waited for news concerning a loved one whose life was hanging in the balance in one of the many operating rooms.

Gladys was a player in the scene, no different from the many other sufferers. She sat numbly waiting for a report regarding her husband's quadruple heart bypass. Gladys and John had been married for more than 30 years. And until five years ago, John had been the picture of health. But then it happened — his first heart attack. Oh, it was only a minor one, which made it a blessing from God. Even the doctor had been positive. "If John will watch his diet and get some exercise, he should be fine."

Those words sent Gladys into high gear. With zeal she began to research heart disease and ways to improve health. She tried to get John to eat the better foods she fixed, to make better food choices during the day, and to exercise daily. But he just couldn't shake his love for meat, potatoes, and the La-Z-Boy recliner!

So, for the past five years, Gladys had nagged John relentlessly and worried herself sick waiting for something more serious to happen. And sure enough, her fears were realized. John did have another attack and had been rushed into surgery that morning. This one was definitely serious — life-threatening!

Gladys' worries were running rampant. "Will John survive the operation? . . . And who's going to pay for this? . . . And will the after-effects of a massive heart attack and major surgery affect his ability to work? . . . And what about John's company? Will they allow him to switch to a less stressful job? . . . And what about my health? I haven't been well myself! I'm a wreck with all this worrying! . . . And will I have to go back to work to support the two of us? . . . And . . ."

On and on the menacing questions poured forth out of Gladys' anxious heart as she sat staring blankly at the TV on the wall, oblivious to what was playing.

WORRY FOR YOUR HUSBAND

Every couple faces and must live through experiences that tempt wives to worry. Unfortunately, worry seems like our time-honored role! And our Gladys is no different. As she sat in that waiting room, she probably reflected back over her three decades of married life. (I would . . . and I have during my own wifely emergency room and surgical waiting room ventures!) Like most married women, Gladys had seen many wonderful times during her years of marriage. But beside her brooding regarding John's health, there had also definitely been other causes for worry and anxiety!

And Gladys is not alone in her worries. I receive a large number of letters and emails daily and also talk regularly to women at my conferences who are dealing with issues in their marriages. Now you may be that rare and exceptional woman who has no problems or who has been able to control your worries. If so, *please* write a book and share your secrets! But for the rest of us, here are some areas where wives tend to worry for and about their husbands.

Health issues. I would have to say health issues are at the top of most wives' list of concerns in a marriage, including my own. If you're young, you and your husband may seem invincible. Please enjoy every minute of such carefree vitality! I smile every time I recall our glorious days of seemingly unlimited energy and abilities. Jim and I camped and sailed — even snow skied once in a while. Then when the children arrived, we rode bikes for 30 miles on Saturdays with a baby seat — and a baby! — on each bike.

But with the passage of time, real and potential health problems will begin to creep into the happy days you enjoy. Aches and pains crop up — some that go away with an aspirin, and others that signal something is wrong. Conditions develop that signal it's time for an altered lifestyle. Maladies arise that call for prescription drugs for the rest of your or your husband's days. Things change as the years mount, and the worries also mount right along with them!

Statistics reveal that most husbands die before their spouses. So like Gladys your husband may be facing serious challenges to his health . . . or they may be just around the corner. Also like Gladys you can only do so much to help your husband deal with his health. And like Gladys you can nag all you want. But if your guy isn't cooperating, or if the changes you've both made don't work, you may end up in a hospital waiting room.

Job issues. We hear of it every day. I'm talking about statistics regarding the rising number of people forced to drop out of college or losing their jobs and joining the new and staggering ranks of the unemployed. Anyone, male or female, who has a job has to be wondering and worrying about the security of their employment. Raises are out of the question. Many companies are keeping their workers but at a lower salary or for less hours — or for more hours while doing the work of two people for no additional pay. Benefits are being reduced as well. Even those who are not affected by cost-cutting measures find themselves doing twice the work . . . and with twice the stress. Fewer and fewer jobholders wake up each day thinking, "I love my work so much, I can hardly wait to get there!"

> *If a couple isn't following God's guidelines for life or being led by the Holy Spirit, disagreements, communication breakdowns, and misunderstandings skyrocket.*

Husbands worry about the stability of work and income, and so do wives! One wife I know who stays at home with a handful of little ones worries about her husband who has been hired to do a singular project. If he meets the deadline, does well, and the project is successful, he gets to keep his job for one more year . . . so he can do another project and possibly keep his job for another year . . . and on and on the outlook goes! This is daily grounds for worry, both his and hers.

Another husband, whose wife is also at home with their young family, has a secure job, but his only chance for a raise is to get more education and pass a battery of exams, competing against an army of other people for the same job position. The pressure's on . . . and so are the reasons for worry.

Still another common scenario for many women is that a wife receives a phone call from her husband, who just left for work an hour ago, saying he's already on his way home. The monthly or quarterly company reports were in, and a certain number of employees were let go that morning . . . and he was one of them. Some couples in this position have been wise with their money and careful with their spending and can make it a few months on funds they've saved in case something like this happened. But, the wife worries, what happens when the money runs out and jobs are next to impossible to land?

I've also heard of *many* instances where a husband has so much stress on the job and concern about the future security of his job and income that he's suffered heart problems or even a heart attack or other physical symptoms spawned by worry.

Few wives are exempt from multiple reasons to be tempted to worry about a husband's job security and income. And every wife probably also worries to a degree about where she fits in the battle for income. If she has been at home, will she have to get a job? Why, she hasn't worked in so long she no longer knows what she could do to supplement their income! Or if she's already working, she's going through the same jitters on her job that her husband is experiencing on his. And, with the latest financial scare, if she's older or took on a job to help through a certain phase of family life, she's wondering, will she ever get to quit? When she started working, it was only supposed to be for a short time. But if her husband loses his job and she keeps hers, what kind of stress will that place on their marriage roles, relationship, and family? I've even talked to many couples where the husband is now a stay-at-home dad, a Mr. Mom. It wasn't their plan or their desire, but it became reality for the sake of survival.

Spiritual issues. For a Christian woman, personal spiritual growth is usually high on her list of goals. But when it comes to her husband's spiritual growth — or lack of it! — well, it can be a stress and worry producer. Why? Because a husband and wife have a bond like no other relationship. What affects one affects the other. And because marriage is the union of two selfish sinners, a good one takes a lot of work on the part of both partners — even for mature and growing Christians. If one of the partners isn't on the same page spiritually but is lagging behind, the marriage — and family! — suffers and is at a great disadvantage. Such a union is like a three-legged stool with one of the legs cut off. Something vital is missing. Without the two partners focused on God and following His guidelines for life, and without the leading of God's Holy Spirit to assist both husband and wife, the opportunities for disagreements, communication breakdowns, and misunderstandings skyrocket.

Gladys is a prime example of this spiritual gulf between a husband and wife. Gladys had always loved God and was faithful over the years to read and study her Bible. Because of her familiarity with God's Word, she was often asked to teach women's Bible classes. In the beginning she was excited and really poured herself into her teaching and rapidly grew spiritually. But there was just one problem. John wasn't where she was spiritually, nor did he want to be. Oh, he had made an effort in the earlier years of their marriage. But as Gladys began to attend Bible studies and even teach several, his initial support and enthusiasm began to wane. After a number of years, Gladys sensed John withdrawing from spiritual matters and involvement as he became intimidated by her growth and enthusiastic participation. Finally he gave up trying to keep up with her. Gladys wanted to be faithful to use her spiritual gifts, but she was worried that her avid church commitments were driving a wedge between her and John.

So as Gladys sat there waiting to see if John would live or die, the questions that had nagged at her for several decades surfaced again: "How do I sustain my marriage and yet faithfully serve God? And if John lives, what can I do to encourage him in the Lord? He needs God's strength and help now more than ever! And if he dies, just how real is his relationship with God? Is he truly a saved believer? Will we know each other in heaven?"

Fidelity issues. Sexual temptation in marriage certainly isn't anything new. (Just read Proverbs 7:6–23, written possibly as far back as 1000 BC — centuries ago!) A wife can't help but worry when her husband leaves the house dressed for business, all polished and shiny, while she's still in her pajamas or sweats. Her worries are amplified as she remembers that his last look at her was with half a bottle of baby food spilled down the front of her less-than-pretty outfit! And it doesn't help to realize he's going to a job where the women are intelligent, successful, and dressed to the hilt. (There's certainly no baby food on any of their up-to-date designer outfits!)

Then there's the temptation of the Internet. Time spent on the Internet, as well as what's viewed on it, is a big problem for men today and giant grounds for worry for wives. Physical temptation in all its forms and avenues is a wife's constant concern for her guy, especially if she's also concerned about his relationship with God. If her husband is wavering spiritually, it generally has an effect on the marriage and the ability to withstand temptation.

Friendship issues. Marriage is a special and unique relationship. In order for it to be alive and vibrant, it requires that both partners continue to work at finding common interests. Remember when you were dating? Both you and your then-future husband made sure you knew what the other liked and made an effort to communicate about a multitude of areas. Socially, you knew the things each other liked and you enjoyed doing them together. But with all that is normal in a marriage — demanding jobs, a house full of kids, grandkids, activities, commitments, parents and in-laws, friends — it's easy to see how distance can develop in a marriage. It becomes harder and harder to get past the necessities of survival and stay in tune with each other.

Gladys had sensed she and John were growing apart in their interests. And she had made an effort to find out some of John's most recent interests. But that hadn't worked. So she gave up . . . at least on the surface. But inside she began to worry that her marriage would end up like so many marriages — with two complete strangers living under the same roof.

As you've been reading this section, maybe you've identified with some or all of the issues and areas I've briefly sketched, or maybe you have a list of your own. But whether it's my list or yours, you and I both need to realize that none of these areas are ultimately under our control. So why do we worry?

WHAT'S A WIFE TO DO?

Life isn't easy, and marriage with its challenges isn't necessarily easy either. Regardless of the many positives that accompany married life, it can sometimes seem as though married life has more issues than we can handle. And so we worry.

Your marriage may be less than ideal. Maybe your husband isn't all that he could and should be. So, you wonder, "What help can I bring to my marriage?" Answer? "Why, I can worry!" That's easy. Worrying is the path that's easiest to take when things aren't going well. But will worrying really help? And *can* it really help? Will it actually motivate and move a husband to work through his struggles? To grow? To be the spiritual leader of the household? We know the answer to those questions, don't we? (And probably we know it from experience!)

So what can we do instead? Abigail in the Old Testament comes to our rescue. She has some solid advice about how we can support our husbands — especially during the difficult times.

Abigail's husband (1 Samuel 25:1–13). Nabal was a rich man, but he was also rude, foolish, ungracious, unsociable, and probably an alcoholic. The Bible actually calls him a "scoundrel" (verse 17), and tells us that his name means "fool" (verse 25). With such a lack of charm, sense, wisdom, and tact, Nabal offended the warrior and future king, David, by refusing to give David's men food after they had protected Nabal's shepherds and flocks. David was so offended over the injustice that he headed out to find Nabal and his household, ready to do great harm to them.

Abigail's actions (1 Samuel 25:14–38). When Abigail heard of Nabal's outrageous treatment of David and his men and learned of David's rage and his plan to annihilate Nabal and all he owned and possessed, she went into action to do what her husband should have done. She gathered the goods David's group needed, brought them to David, and threw herself at his feet. There she begged for his grace, hoping to defuse the volatile, life-threatening situation. When she returned from delivering the supplies and pacifying David's anger, she found her husband holding a drunken feast, totally oblivious to his foolish social blunder. Sensing that speaking to her husband when he was drunk was not the best timing, she wisely waited until morning to give him a report so he could take in the information and grasp the gravity of the situation.

Abigail's example. First of all, how would you have handled the situation — the snub and the disrespectful treatment of a powerful and upright man who had done a good deed? Would you have paced the floor, anxiously hoping your husband would wise up? Would you have wrung your hands or pulled out your hair? And how would you have handled telling your husband about the situation and results afterward, especially after finding him so carefree and oblivious to his error? Would you have yelled, lectured, called him names (stupid, idiot, klutz, imbecile, fool), or degraded him with your words?

We can learn a valuable lesson — or two! — from Abigail. What did she do? In one word, she showed "discretion." Abigail's wisdom saved the day. She realized the problem her husband had created. He had definitely made a wrong decision that almost cost him everything, including his life, property, and the lives of his wife and their innocent servants. But Abigail acted quickly and carefully. She exhibited good judgment in her timing, her choice of words, and her manner. Her response, actions, and choice of words — both to David and her husband — were effective and helped disarm a potentially disastrous situation.

The point of Abigail's story is that you can help your husband even when he doesn't necessarily want your help. And guess what?

Such help doesn't come from worrying. No, it comes from wisdom — wise decisions, wise actions, and wise words, all guided by God in answer to your *prayers,* not your *worrying!* You just need to be discreet. Major on asking God for help and acting on His direction rather than on anxiety.

Doing Your Part

Marriage is a team effort. Sometimes a team (whether it's a sports team or a debate team or a corporate team . . . or a marriage team) fails to function as a unit. When this happens, its performance is hampered. Oh, the members go through the motions and do what they're supposed to do, but they fail to win. They miss the opportunity to celebrate the triumph only a team effort can bring. Well, marriage is like that. It's a team! You can't make your other team member — your husband — do anything. So instead of giving in to worry, do what you can to help and honor him. Whether it's his refusal to take his health seriously (as Gladys experienced) or his misuse of time, money, or a hundred other things, do your part.

✓ *Stop worrying about your husband's*

faults. Quit being so anxious about all that you think is wrong with your husband. Instead, start focusing on what's right about him. And go a step further — express it to him! Work at changing your perspective. When you married, he was a wonderful guy in your eyes. And with a change of attitude from you, the wonderful old him just might reemerge! Constantly think back on those things that attracted you to your husband in the first place. Also consciously notice what he does that's right, that's helpful, that's commendable. And don't forget to compliment him and share what you've noticed.

> *If you're worried about an area in your husband's life, talk to God . . . and then talk to your man honestly and openly.*

✓ *Step up your prayers for your husband.* It's hard to criticize someone you're praying for. So pray. You can't pray too much, but you can certainly pray too little. Pray specifically for your areas of concern. Embrace prayer for your husband as a lifelong commitment. When things begin to turn around in one area, thank God . . . and then move to the next area of concern.

✓ *Talk to your husband.* Most marriage counselors will tell you that if a husband and wife will talk to each other, they can solve any problem in their marriage. If you find yourself worrying about an area in your husband's life, ask God to show you areas where you may be contributing to the problem. Next, follow Abigail's example and use discretion. Check your actions. Check your timing. Check your words. Above all, check your heart. Then ask your husband how you can help or how you can change.

Breaking the Worry Habit . . . Forever!

As a married woman, my closest friend and companion is my husband. Jim and I traveled through the beginnings of a fresh young marriage and experienced the addition of children, seeing them grow up, marry, and begin their own families. This was all natural and good. And such a natural and good progression leaves a couple as a twosome again for most of their days. So as a wife, who's left to worry about? Who's number one on my "People to Worry About" list? Why it's my husband, the other part of the team I belong to! And, as you well know, there's plenty to worry about!

Whatever stage of married life you're in as you read this chapter, take heart! You *can* conquer your natural tendency to worry. You *can* break the worry habit. I sincerely hope and pray you will choose to head down a better path so you don't suffer your own personal physical repercussions caused by anxiety. You don't have to be a nailbiter, a hand wringer, a pacer, or a nervous wreck. And you don't have to develop migraine headaches or bleeding ulcers or deep furrows in your brow. No, you can form godly habits that nip worrying in the bud and keep it from growing into a full-blown weed, a bona fide worry habit.

It boils down to asking, "Am I willing to obey God's commands not to worry? Am I willing to trust God instead of worrying? Am I willing to trade in my fretting for God's promised strength, His wisdom, and His peace that passes understanding?" Do as David did. He declared, "I sought the LORD, and He heard me, and delivered me from all my fears" (Psalm 34:4). Seek the Lord. That's your part in overcoming worry. And His part? God will hear you . . . *and* deliver you from all your fears.

The righteous cry out, and the LORD hears,
and delivers them out of all their troubles.
PSALM 34:17

4
DO YOU KNOW WHERE YOUR CHILDREN ARE?

Train up a child in the way he should go.
PROVERBS 22:6

It's only been 15 minutes, but Pam is a nervous wreck already! She has worried about this moment for 16 years, and it's finally arrived! Her precious 16-year-old daughter, Julie, is out on her first-ever official date. Bill, Julie's date, seemed like a nice young man. And he had followed all the standards and requirements set down by Julie's dad, Fred. Bill had called Fred and asked to take Julie out. The event was at the high school and was to be heavily chaperoned. Bill, like Julie, was a newly licensed driver. Therefore the couple agreed to go from Point A (home) to Point B (the school) and return to Point A as soon as the event was over. Still Pam couldn't help but fret.

Parenting certainly hadn't been easy for Pam and Fred. In fact, where their older son was concerned, it could even be labeled "failure" or "disaster." Jack had been a handful at home from Day 1. And even now that he was gone, he continued to give them much heartache. Jack had married very early against Pam and Fred's expressed wishes. This had put a strain on their relationship not only with the daughter-in-law but also with Jack. Initially their parental concerns seemed to be unwarranted. And within a year, Pam's first grandbaby, little Samantha — Sam for short — was born. What joy! Sam was the cutest little thing! All was rosy.

But now, two years later, the bottom had dropped out of the young couple's rocky marriage, and there was even talk of divorce. To make matters worse, Jack refused to talk to Pam and Fred, and their daughter-in-law had stopped letting Pam see little Sam. Sam's — and Jack's — future was yet another of Pam's constant worries and heartaches.

So there she sat in her living room . . . worrying. Pam worried constantly about a grown son and a grandbaby on one side of town and a daughter just entering the world of "boys" and dating whom she hoped was safe on the other side of town at the high school. And then there was worry at home-sweet-home where Jason, her younger son, sat upstairs behind his permanently closed bedroom door. Jason was only nine, but already he was forever on the computer. *There's so much garbage on the Internet! Who knows what in the world he's being exposed to day after day!* Pam thought.

Pam's worry cup was definitely filled to overflowing . . . and spilling out in every direction at once. Truly, her children provided a literal lifetime of opportunities for worry!

Moms Love to Worry About Danger

It's hard in this day and age not to worry about the well-being of your children . . . and grandchildren. We live in a world that's dangerous on all fronts. Of course you do your best to protect your children. But it's also true that you can't keep them sheltered at home forever. And when they leave your house, anxiety in no way lets up. Out of sight is definitely not out of mind! No, quite the opposite, the possibilities for worry escalate, multiply, and skyrocket!

For thousands of years moms have fretted over the possibilities of danger for their children. Take, for instance, one Old Testament mom, Hagar. (You can read her story in Genesis 21:8–21.) Her worry was in no way imaginary. No, it was for real! In spite of all her efforts and care for the welfare and protection of her only child, her son, Ishmael, Hagar ended up watching over him as he lay dying of thirst in the desert and listening to his agonizing cries as he suffered. She and her son had been sent away from the safety and protection of the patriarch Abraham's care. Abraham was the boy's father, but his wife, Sarah, wanted Hagar and Ishmael out of their lives and home. So Abraham sent them away. Hagar was totally on her own in the vastness of a killer desert . . . which led to their perilous condition.

You may or may not be able to identify with this story in its harsh life-or-death reality, but at some time most mothers experience worry and fear about the physical condition of their children, beginning as early as pregnancy. In spite of their best efforts, the child or children find themselves in harm's way or in danger because of time spent with the wrong crowd . . . or a life-threatening medical condition . . . or a drunk or hit-

and-run driver . . . or an accident at home, school, a friend's house, camp, or on a basketball court. All of these possibilities and realities — and more! — give moms opportunities for some serious worry.

> *Your heavenly Father is a loving and compassionate God who loves you and your children.*

Perhaps, like Hagar, your fears and tears are justified. Like her, you may have a child who is in a serious or life-threatening situation. But as you read Hagar's story, notice something else that's also true for you — God was aware of the boy's situation. "The angel of God called to Hagar out of heaven . . . 'Fear not'" (verse 17). God then acted and provided water. He also gave a prophecy of hope regarding the lad's future: "I will make him a great nation" (verse 18).

In our own time of being parents and grandparents, Jim and I have gone through the birth of a grandchild with a physical defect and the ensuing corrective surgery and treatment, the hospitalization of another grandchild in an emergency situation, and a daughter's bout with a malignant tumor and all that entails. Each one of these crises was alarming. Each one was easy grounds for sickening worry. Each one forced me to do battle with worry and press myself closer to God through prayer. And each one grew in me a greater trust in God's plan and His promised love and care for me *and* my afflicted family members.

These were real conditions and real trouble that came my way. And I'm sure my family is not done with trials and tribulations that cause one's heart to stop and pound at the same time. Life truly is filled with opportunities around every corner to worry about the health and welfare of our offspring!

Legitimate concern will always be part of the very nature of a mom. So will attention to safety and basic emergency skills. Looking out for our kids is one of our responsibilities and assignments from God. We're to be like the mother in Proverbs 31:27, who "watches over the ways of her household," and that includes the children! But always remember, God is aware of your child's situation. He is also a loving and compassionate God. You can cease worrying, pry your fingers away from your hold on your children, and count on God. Diligently and faithfully do your part, but trust God for His part. As with Hagar, more times than not, your children's safety is out of your control. So rather than worry, choose to pray and put their physical safety into the loving hands of God.

MOMS LOVE TO WORRY ABOUT SUCCESS

If you're like me, you want your children to have some of the things you didn't have when you were growing up. And you certainly don't want them to make the same mistakes you did. Put another way, you want them to have a better life, to *live* a better life. In short, you're ambitious, or desirous of their success. But beware! Such ambition can backfire. Sadly, Rebekah is an illustration of this reality.

Rebekah had two sons. The youngest — Jacob — was clearly her favorite. She wanted her little Jacob, who had become a grown man, to receive the blessing that was due her older son, Esau. This couldn't have been a spur-of-the-moment thought on Rebekah's part. No, she knew the custom of the "firstborn" receiving the legal birthright and blessings from the father. However, when the time was right, Rebekah hatched a devious plan to secure the success she wished for Jacob. In her concern for the financial welfare of her favorite son, she was willing to break God's plan and rules in favor of her own (Genesis 27:1–13).

Are you worried about the social and financial status of your children? Many moms worry about their children going to the "best" schools, living in the "best" neighborhood, meeting the "right" people for the connections needed to get ahead. This is basically what Rebekah did. She manipulated her favored son, her husband, and her less-favored son in order to advance her ambitious desires for Jacob's "best" — for his position, wealth, and welfare.

And what was the result? Jacob had to literally run for his life. He was forced to flee from his home to avoid the murderous wrath of his brother. Sadly, Rebekah never saw her precious Jacob again.

What do you imagine the family situation would have been like in the face of a lifetime of partiality and deception and after something as drastic as one son seeking to murder the other, leading to a family split? If it was bad before such a rift, it could only have been worse afterward. Most likely, it was unbearable.

Rebekah's aspirations for her son moved her to take matters into her own hands and created a family disaster. Dreaming about bettering your children's lives is not a bad thing. You should want to make sure your children are properly educated and develop self-discipline and self-motivation.

You should want your children to succeed and contribute positively to society and their future families. But you should never desire these things at the expense of godly principles. Focus your attention on training your children in righteousness. Show them the way — and the why — of making choices that please God. Then pray faithfully and trust the Lord to lead them and give them direction for their future careers, jobs, and marriage partners. In the words of Jesus, "Seek first the kingdom of God and His righteousness, and all these things shall be added to you" (Matthew 6:33).

MOMS LOVE TO WORRY ABOUT SPIRITUAL GROWTH

Not too long ago I talked with a pastor's wife who was worried sick about the spiritual condition of her son. He was about 12 years old and had yet to open his heart to Christ as Savior. The boy had been in church all his life, and his mom was worried that he would never acknowledge and accept Christ as the Lord and Master of his life. This loving, caring mom had tied herself in knots with worry for her son.

It's a good thing — and natural — to be concerned for the spiritual condition of our children. The apostle Paul had a fervent ongoing interest in the spiritual standing of his "children" in Christ. He begged them to "no longer be children tossed to and fro and carried about with every wind of doctrine, by the trickery of men, in the cunning craftiness of deceitful plotting" (Ephesians 4:14).

John too was deeply desirous that his "children" follow God's ways. To them he wrote, "I have no greater joy than to hear that my children walk in truth" (3 John 3).

The caring father in Proverbs 1 instructed and appealed to his child, "My son, if sinners entice you, do not consent . . . Do not walk in the way with them, keep your foot from their path" (verses 10 and 15).

What can you do with your love and concern for your children? And what can you do to help move your children's spiritual maturity along? Paul shows us the way. He had a choice to make. He could either worry himself sick, or he could do something about his concerns. And that's exactly what he did. He tackled and went after the spiritual issues of his "children" head-on. He wrote passionate letters to them addressing their failures, shortcomings, and lack of wisdom and their need for spiritual growth. Here are some of his concerns:

✂ They were spiritually immature — *I, brethren, could not speak to you as to spiritual people but as to carnal, as to babes in Christ* (1 Corinthians 3:1).

✂ They were too friendly with the world — *Do not be unequally yoked together with unbelievers. For what fellowship has righteousness with lawlessness?* (2 Corinthinas 6:14).

✂ They were failing to follow God — *Oh foolish Galatians! Who has bewitched you that you should not obey the truth?* (Galatians 3:1).

Paul preached on paper, but he also prayed. With a heart overflowing with love, he prayed:

[I pray] that you may be filled with the knowledge of His will in all wisdom and spiritual understanding; that you may walk worthy of the Lord, fully pleasing Him, being fruitful in every good work, and increasing in the knowledge of God, strengthened with all might, according to His glorious power (Colossians 1:9–11).

Along the parenting path I'm sure you'll

be expressing some of these same passionate appeals to your children and to God. I certainly have! You *should* speak up when your child's spiritual condition is at risk. Proverbs 27:5–6 encourages us to voice our concerns in the name of love: "Open rebuke is better than love carefully concealed. Faithful are the wounds of a friend." In other words, love speaks up. Love cares. Love even goes to the mat! Just be sure you look up and pray first so what you say is said with a heart of love and words of wisdom. "The wisdom that is from above is first pure, then peaceable, gentle, willing to yield, full of mercy and good fruits, without partiality and without hypocrisy" (James 3:17).

My point is that you and I should care enough to lovingly point out what we're seeing in our kids that doesn't match up with God's instructions and standards. But . . . we also need to stop worrying! We need to use the same time and energy worrying requires to pray and prepare our children to walk with God and do spiritual battle, to fight the good fight of faith and live for Christ.

We, the parents, and they, the children, "do not wrestle against flesh and blood, but against principalities, against powers, against the rulers of the darkness of this age, against spiritual hosts of wickedness in the heavenly places" (Ephesians 6:12). So your job is to do all you can to help your children "put on the whole armor of God, that [they] may be able to stand against the wiles of the devil" (verse 11).

Doing Your Part

Worrying about your children only makes matters worse for you and your health and peace of mind. It also increases tension in your family relationships and in the atmosphere at home. And it is a deterrent to your spiritual growth. The "fruit of the Spirit" — the evidence that you are filled with the Spirit and walking in Christlikeness — "is love, joy, peace, longsuffering, kindness, goodness, faithfulness, gentleness, self-control" (Galatians 5:22–23). Worry is not a part of this list of godly behavior, and it has no part in God's plan or His will. Therefore worry is not to be a part of your daily life. It's only when you start trusting God and seeking His help and take right actions and begin doing something about your children, their lives, and their issues that things will begin to change positively. Here are a few things you can start doing right now!

✓ *Pray for your children.* I'm sure this is a given on your part. But honestly, when things aren't going well, I tend to worry more and more and pray less and less fervently for my children and grand-children. It's almost an either/or scenario. Either I worry or I pray. I can't do both at the same time! It's easier to succumb to anxiety than it is to calm down, shove worry aside, and let my fears and requests be made known to God.

To make sure I pray for my kids and grandkids, I put their names on a prayer list. When things are going well and I'm tempted to pray less — or less fervently — for them, their names are right there staring me in the face. Then when trying times return, I'm in the habit of praying, ready immediately to pray for the difficulties in their lives. I've learned to beware of failing to pray during the "good times" . . . which leads me to worry less.

> *The more you're with or near your kids, the more they'll know you're available and willing to listen.*

Are you concerned for who your children might marry? Jim and I were, so we started praying about this when our girls were little. What are your concerns for your kids? What are you worrying about? Start — and continue — praying faithfully for their lives and choices. Follow Job's example. God reports Job "would rise early in the morning and offer burnt offerings according to the number of them all [his children]. For Job said, 'It may be that my sons have sinned and cursed God in their hearts.' Thus Job did regularly" (Job 1:5). Dear mom, never forget that "the effective, fervent prayer of a righteous man [or mom] avails much" (James 5:16).

✓ *Be available to your children.* I don't know about you, but I could never orchestrate discussions with my daughters as they were growing up. Some of our most open and honest talks happened when I was just there. It's only as we spent time together that my girls opened up and started talking. And you know, it's still that way today. Often when I'm with them, a pause in their hyperbusy lives will occur and there will be a chance for us to talk, even if it's side-by-side as I help them with a baby, a meal, the dishes, or housework. Such times give me the opportunity to put in my two cents' worth of advice based on experience . . . and always a mountain full of encouragement and praise! Now that doesn't mean you and I have to be our children's "best friend." It means we must make it a point to be near or with them often, so they know we are available if and when they need us. (P.S. I don't live in the same state as either of my daughters. This means that to have time together, I have to plan ahead, block out time, and put out some money. But, of course, in the in-between times I practice long-distance love. I text, email, call, and mail them little gifts.)

✓ *Prepare your children.* You can help protect your children from the world and its evils by faithfully instructing them from God's Word. The Bible is the ultimate book of wisdom, advice, and information about the dangers of being in the wrong places or with the wrong people, about good habits, and about sexual purity. Help your children understand that God protects them not only through His providence but also through their obedience in following His instructions in His Word, the Bible.

✓ *Guard your children.* Your children are a stewardship from God. That means He has given them to *you* and assigned *you* to watch over, instruct, and train them. They are a precious commodity, which means you have a long-term responsibility to provide strong parental leadership. Notice I said "long-term" responsibility. Many parents tend to provide less direction as their children get older. Yet it is my own personal opinion, and the experience of other parents as well as that of Jim and me, that as our kids grow older, they require more direct input, not less. You'll need to continue to closely monitor your children's decisions and their use of time, TV, and the Internet, as well as movies, friends, and dating relationships.

If you're worried about your children, don't. Instead take action. Do something about it. The first thing you can do is acknowledge worry for what it is — useless . . . and a sin. Then turn fully to God. If you've become lax as a parent, admit it to Him and ask for His strength to live out your role as a parent, a mom. Make fresh "mom commitments" to Him, and put them in writing. Next, seek the help or counsel you need. There is wisdom, confidence, and power in a multitude of counselors. "By wise counsel wage war" (Proverbs 20:18). Talk things over with Dad and try to agree on the actions you can take. Then take the time to provide a closer level of parental guidance. This will take time, and you may have to cut out a few of your favorite activities. But don't you agree the spiritual and physical welfare of your children is worth it? If you're unsure what to do, pray this prayer uttered from the heart of Paul, "Lord, what do You want me to do?" (Acts 9:6).

Breaking the Worry Habit . . . Forever!

Speaking of habits, here's a good one to nurture. Make it a habit to turn your worries for your children into opportunities for you not only to trust God but to think of ways to instruct and prepare your kids for the areas of danger that cause you concern.

Do your part to train them to follow God and seek His will for their lives and future. Your goal — and role — is to train them to make godly decisions on their own. God's Word says you're to "train up a child in the way he should go" (Proverbs 22:6). To do this calls for a decision, a commitment, and lots of effort . . . for a long time! . . . on your part.

Just think how long your own training in the "path of righteousness" has taken! And, if you're like me, you still have some areas of weakness. So be patient with your children. Be an encourager — their Number One Encourager. If you get a little exasperated with their growth (or lack of it!), look in a mirror and realize God isn't finished with you either. Then, when you've done your instructing, training, and praying, entrust your darlings into the completely capable, all-powerful, loving hands of God. He loves them even more than you do and cares about their growth in Christ even more than you do. It may take years — even decades — for the things you're praying about and teaching them today and all along the way to bear fruit. But be faithful to do your part. Then leave the results to God. And, of course, continue to pray, pray, pray for your precious ones until your last dying breath.

*Now may the Lord of peace Himself
give you peace always in every way.
The Lord be with you.*

2 THESSALONIANS 3:16

5
I'M 30 AND STILL SINGLE!

But as God has distributed to each one,
as the Lord has called each one,
so let him walk.

1 CORINTHIANS 7:17

As the final lesson in her quarterly Bible study featuring 1 Corinthians chapters 1 through 6 was wrapping up, Claire reflected back on the many marvelous evenings she had spent studying God's Word with a great group of like-minded single career gals. She had learned soooo much, and she sensed God was doing a great work in her heart and changing her thinking and behavior in many areas. But still, there was a restless unsettledness in her spirit. "Oh, well," she shrugged, "maybe dessert will help." With that Claire temporarily dismissed her uneasiness and turned to sweeter things!

The women in the study all helped themselves to Yolanda's homemade brownies and sat back down for their weekly prayer and share time. First, Jill asked for prayer for her mom who was going through cancer treatments and wasn't a believer. Then there was Carlotta, who was having trouble with the godless atmosphere at her work. Then came silence as everyone waited to see who would share next. Time seemed to be on pause as Claire struggled with whether she should say anything or not. Her pressing issue seemed so trivial compared to the other concerns. But Claire's heart was breaking, and she could contain herself no longer. She blurted out, "Next week when we meet will be my birthday. And . . ."

Before Claire could even get to her actual request, the group swung immediately into action. "Hey, everyone! Who'll bring a cake?" shouted one of Claire's friends. "I'll bring some balloons!" Each woman had some suggestions of how to make Claire's birthday a special occasion, including instructions for everyone to bring a gift under $5.

"No! No! Stop all this!" Claire couldn't believe her ears as she heard her voice crescendo. "You don't understand! This isn't a good thing! There's nothing to celebrate. I'm going to be 30 and I'm still single! Please pray for me."

GOD'S PERSPECTIVE ON SINGLENESS

Poor Claire. Her worries over her singleness were affecting a perfectly good opportunity to enjoy a party and some fun with her caring and loving friends (not to mention how her concerns were affecting her attitude and behavior!). She had been an absolute bear for the past six months as she fretted over what she perceived to be a negative situation. If she had just read ahead into the next chapter of 1 Corinthians, Claire would have received an extremely affirming and encouraging message from God about her singleness. She would have learned God's positive perspective on her unmarried status.

As we take a peek at 1 Corinthians 7, realize the apostle Paul was writing a letter to the church at Corinth, a church he had planted several years earlier on his second missionary journey. (See Acts 18:1–18.) In chapters 1 through 6 he had addressed many problems the church was facing. Then he turned to giving practical answers to some questions people in the congregation were asking. The first of these questions had to do with marriage. This was a hot topic of concern due to the morally corrupt nature of the Corinthian culture where these Christians lived. True, Paul was writing to the folks in Corinth almost 2000 years ago, but he was also writing to Claire and other singles today. He had a few key principles to share regarding marriage and singleness. Hear now the wisdom of God through Paul.

> *One of the greatest advantages of singleness is the potential for greater focus on Christ and accomplishing work for Him.*

Singleness and marriage are both gifts from God. Many unmarried adults feel tremendous pressure and an overwhelming desire to be married. They think their lives cannot be complete if they remain single. However, the Bible says differently. Paul, who is believed to have been single, wrote, "I wish that all men were even as I myself [that is, unmarried]. But each one has his own gift from God, one in this manner and another in that" (verse 7). According to Scripture, Claire and other singles need to understand that neither marriage nor singleness is morally better than the other. Both are worthy and valuable avenues for accomplishing God's purposes (verses 1–9).

Singleness is a calling from God. Paul continues to instruct those who are discontent with their present situation of marriage or singleness: "But as God has distributed to each one, as the Lord has called each one, so let him walk" (verse 17). Many of the new believers in Corinth were unhappy (like Claire!) about their life situations (verses 7–24). Some wanted to change their marital status. Some who were slaves wanted to be free. Others wanted to use their freedom in Christ as opportunities to sin. Paul gives them God's response to their discontentment: Christians should willingly and happily accept where God has placed them. If they are married, they are to stay married. If they are single, they are to accept singleness until — and if — it becomes obvious God wants them to marry. And if they're slaves, they are to accept their social condition. Why? Because God has placed them in these roles and situations to serve His purposes. They are to stay in these situations until it is clear God is leading them in another direction.

Singleness allows freedom to serve God. One of the greatest advantages of singleness is the potential for a greater focus on Christ and His work. A single woman doesn't have the responsibility of caring for a husband and raising a family. Therefore she can serve God and His people to her heart's content! She can go on mission trips. She can have a hotline into her apartment and counsel until the wee hours of the morning. She can be at the church every time the door opens and serve the people in her local church in a multitude of ways. However, a married woman is to focus her priority time, energy, and attention on her husband and children, which limits her service to others beyond her family circle. Yes, she serves and participates at church, but in a greatly reduced capacity. The Bible explains the difference in this way: "The unmarried woman cares about the things of the Lord, that she may be holy both in body and in spirit. But she who is married cares about the things of the world — how she may please her husband" (verse 34).

Hopefully when Claire reads 1 Corinthians 7 for her next Bible study meeting, she'll realize that singleness is not a bad thing. In fact, it's a good thing! Why worry? And especially, why worry about a *good* thing? Just think . . . a wide-open path is right in front of Claire and every other woman who's single. So she has a choice to make. She can continue to worry and fret, be frustrated and disgruntled around others, and limit her usefulness to Christ and His people. Or she can accept her singleness, answer God's call, and step through His open door to full-out service to Him and His people. Happiness, joy, usefulness, and fulfillment are all hers whenever she chooses to settle down into her life situation and wholeheartedly serve the Lord.

As I think of the many dear women in the Bible who accepted the challenge to serve others and not stall out in their singleness, I'm first reminded of Moses' sister, Miriam. As an unmarried woman, Miriam led the Israelite women in a song of deliverance after the Egyptians had drowned in the Red Sea (Exodus 15:20–21). Evidently she played an important role in this delivery because the prophet Micah states that God delivered Israel by the hand of "Moses, Aaron, and

Miriam" (Micah 6:4). She also was the first woman to be given the title of "prophetess" (Exodus 15:20). Rather than focus on her singleness, Miriam focused on her service. Because she was unencumbered by marriage and family, she was free to fully serve God, His people, and her brothers. She had a vital ministry alongside her two famous brothers!

Then there are the four daughters of Philip the evangelist. They were single and prophetesses who seemed to have an ongoing prophetic ministry. Acts 21:9 reports, "Now this man [Philip] had four virgin daughters who prophesied." These unmarried sisters were called by God for a special ministry and actively participated in God's work.

And we can't forget Lydia! She is an outstanding model for all women of devotion, commitment, service, assistance, giving, and hospitality. It's believed she too was unmarried. As the apostle Paul preached the gospel of Christ, "the Lord opened her heart to heed the things spoken by Paul" (Acts 16:14). From the moment of salvation, Lydia served! She invited Paul and his coworkers to make her home their headquarters. In time her home became the meeting place of the local church. Her service, generosity, and hospitality did much to advance the church in Philippi. She was a businesswoman — a seller of purple goods — but she made God's work her business as well.

WIDOWS AND WORRY

A vast group of singles are widows. They come in all ages, from newlyweds to octogenarians and beyond, and every age in between. Let's face it, most married women will outlive their husbands and one day become widows. That's what statistics tell us, and that's one reason we worry.

But worry begins *way* before a spouse's death! Here's how the worry progression usually goes. As a single, a woman worries about not being married. Then when she meets the right man and gets married, she quickly shifts her energies to worrying about her newest project — her husband — and concentrates her worries on his job, his health, his spiritual growth, his parenting, his fidelity, his friends. On and on goes the "Things to Worry About Regarding My Husband" list. She even worries about his death and her years of widowhood. But is this the way it should be? No, not at all. Instead of worrying about her husband's death — when he is happy and healthy and right beside her enjoying a wonderful life — a wife should give thanks to God daily. She should serve and savor her sweetheart fully. Then, if and when she does become a widow, she can, in her singleness, completely count on God for all her needs.

A widow can count on God for her care. God is faithful. Faithfulness is His nature, one of His divine attributes. And hasn't He said, "I will never leave you nor forsake you" (Hebrews 13:5)? Therefore a widow can trust God for all her needs. She can be comforted by these truths and promises about God, her heavenly Father *and* her new husband ("for your Maker is your husband" — Isaiah 54:5):

✿ *The LORD watches over the strangers; He relieves the fatherless and widow* (Psalm 146:9).

✿ *The LORD will destroy the house of the proud, but He will establish the boundary of the widow* (Proverbs 15:25).

✿ *Now she who is really a widow, and left alone, trusts in God* (1 Timothy 5:5).

A widow can count on God's people for care. God's people are a family, right? And what do members of a caring family do?

They watch out for each other. Widows can be comforted by God's instructions to the church to "honor widows who are really widows" (1 Timothy 5:3). Her immediate family is assigned to be the initial provider of her care (verses 4 and 16). And her church family can and should also assist her with her daily needs (verse 9).

WIDOWS AND SERVICE

Like other singles, a widow has a choice to make. She can worry about her situation as a widow, or she can take up God's challenge and take on the multitude of opportunities that are hers for service. Depending on her age and whether or not she has children at home, she can shift her service from her husband's needs to the church's needs. Like my husband's mother, Lois, who was widowed twice, a widow can gain a reputation with her service, being "well reported for good works," offering hospitality to others, caring for people in need, and diligently following every good work (verse 10).

The Bible shows us many marvelous examples of widows who contributed significantly to God's purposes and people.

Ruth. One of the most-loved stories in the Old Testament is that of the young widow

Ruth. After the death of her husband, she made a decision to follow her mother-in-law, Naomi, back to Israel. Naomi freely gave Ruth the option of going back to her own people and possibly remarrying. In fact, Naomi told her to! But Ruth chose instead to go with Naomi and serve and take care of her dead husband's mother. I'm inspired by her classic resolve every time I read this declaration of her devotion:

Entreat me not to leave you, or to turn back from following after you; for wherever you go, I will go; and wherever you lodge, I will lodge; your people shall be my people, and your God, my God (Ruth 1:16).

The widow of Zarephath — During a time of severe famine in the land of Israel, this single mom and widow gave up her last bit of food to feed God's prophet Elijah. In response to her faith, obedience, and sacrifice, God provided food for her and her son during the famine (1 Kings 17:9–16).

Anna. This amazing woman had been married for seven years and then lived as a widow until she was 84 years old. Then one glorious day the infant Jesus was brought to the temple by His parents — the temple where the widow Anna worshiped God. Anna "did not depart from the temple, but served God with fastings and prayers night and day" (Luke 2:37). God honored Anna's faithful service by allowing her the blessing of seeing the Messiah in her lifetime.

The widow who gave all. One day when Jesus was in the temple He observed those who were placing their tithes into the treasury. True to form, the rich gave much. But Jesus called together His disciples and pointed out a poor widow who dropped in only "two mites," about one-eighth of a penny. Jesus commended this destitute widow's giving, explaining:

This poor widow has put in more than all those who have given to the treasury; for they all put in out of their abundance, but she out of her poverty put in all that she had, her whole livelihood (Mark 12:43–44).

A group of modern-day servants. At my former church, a group of widows turned up at church whenever there was a need, whether it was the Monday morning prayer group, the Tuesday morning sorting of Sunday's visitor cards, the Wednesday morning women's Bible study, or . . . I think you get the picture! Whenever and wherever service was required or a need was made evident, these ladies stepped in to help. I have to tell you, whenever one of these dear widowed saints went home to be with the Lord, we as a church body felt her absence.

I mentioned Jim's mom earlier. Lois was a member of this group of serving widowed saints. In fact, Lois was one of its ringleaders. How tragic it would have been for our church if any one of these precious ladies had chosen to sit on the sidelines feeling sorry for herself or preoccupying herself with the cares of this world.

Doing Your Part

Perhaps you are single, a single mom, or a widow. If so, here are a few things to add to your to-do list.

✓ *Embrace your singleness.* For a life of joy and confidence, welcome God's plan for you at this time in your life. Relish your status as a single and reap the blessings that come from accepting God's will. Please don't resist God's calling. Don't be like Jonah in the Old Testament, who worked against God's purposes by trying to run from His will. You have choices to make. You can worry yourself sick. You can fret or chafe against your situation. You can be angry and frustrated, even bitter. Like our friend Claire, you can try to make everyone else as miserable as you are. You can even try to manipulate your way out of singleness and end up marrying the "wrong" person.

Beloved, I'm not in your position, but I may be someday, so I'm taking this advice to heart as well. As you and I look at God and acknowledge His

> *Be available. Opportunities for ministry will probably land on your doorstep every day.*

providence, His sovereignty, His wisdom, and His all-knowing character, it seems that the right and God-honoring thing to do is to accept His good and acceptable and perfect will for you at this time. His choice is always the best choice!

✓ *Own your role.* What a wonderful thing to know your purpose! So many Christians search and search for it. But you, if you're single, know yours. And it is a glorious one! Just as a married woman has a purpose, so do you! A married woman serves her husband and children . . . and then the people in the church with her additional time and energy. However, you get the honor and privilege of unencumbered service to your Lord! You get to pull out all the stops and serve to your heart's content. So please don't miss out on this most rewarding role! Develop your spiritual gifts and ask those in leadership at your church about areas of ministry where you could help others and use your time and gifts. Begin by just being available. You probably won't even have to look for opportunities for ministry. Amazingly, they'll land on your doorstep every day!

✓ *Keep yourself pure.* God keys in on being "holy both in body and in spirit" (1 Corinthians 7:34). God is holy, holy, holy, and those who serve Him are to fight the battle of keeping themselves untainted and pure from sin. Devotion to God encompasses devotion to holiness in body and in spirit. To be dedicated to God includes the dedication of body and spirit. As one who is striving to please God, you must also be striving to be pure. You are God's and you belong to God. Your situation as a single gives you the opportunity for greater focus on Christ and His work and many special opportunities to serve Him wholeheartedly. Your role is to not allow sin to disqualify you from such service.

✓ *Encourage those who are single.* Married or single, every woman can be an encourager to those who are single. For three years my primary ministry was to the single career adult women in my church. My Jim pastored them, and I flung open my heart and the doors of our home to this fantastic flock of women. Wow, it was a rich ministry. Every Wednesday night I led a Bible study for this group in my home. We grew together. We studied God's Word together. We shared our lives with each other. We prayed for one another. We created fun outings and get-togethers.

There I was, a haggard wife, mother of two girls, and homemaker. We even had to wait until the girls were in bed to begin our study. Some of the women would arrive and express how much they wanted what I had — a husband, children, and a home. And there I stood in all my tiredness, wishing I had their freedom, their energy, their free time, their commitment to a variety of ministries . . . on and on my envy list went. They were gold! While I was stuck at home, they were professionals in the workplace. They were hip and up-to-date. God was first in their lives, even as they worked in the world. They rarely missed an evening, did their study during the week, and prayed faithfully. They were always planning greater ways to reach out and be involved in witnessing for Christ. They constantly brought friends from work and their apartment complexes to church. They volunteered whenever there was a need. Honestly, I miss them!

I could tell you more about this great group, but my point is, dear reader, *you* can play a vital role in helping singles who would benefit from someone like you coming alongside them and letting them know how much you appreciate and admire them for their ministries and accomplishments. I know that because that's what I was doing. You see, "Claire" was in my Bible study!

Breaking the Worry Habit . . . Forever!

Believe me, habits are so hard to break. Here I am writing a book on worry, and I woke up this morning worrying about something I must face next week, five days away! So whether you are single or not, something is always going on — or not going on! — in your life to feed the worry habit. But as we end this chapter on singleness, I hope you are grasping the reassuring reality of God's plan for you if you are presently single, or if you become single in the future. Why worry about singleness? As in all things, God's got you covered . . . no matter what happens, where you are, or what your life involves.

Let your conduct be without covetousness; be content with such things as you have.
HEBREWS 13:5

6
WHY DO I HAVE TO BE THE RESPONSIBLE ONE?

And Jesus answered and said to her, "Martha, Martha, you are worried and troubled about many things."
LUKE 10:41

As Ann Marie picked over her lunch during her break, she stared at her to-do list . . .

"Let's see," she sighed as she braced herself for the awful truth. "After work I need to run by the mall and shop for birthday gifts for the twins, look for a graduation present for my niece, exchange that pair of jeans for Bobbie, and select a birthday card for my sister. Then I need to pick up the cleaning and stop at the grocery store to get something to make for dinner tonight. And . . . oh, no! What was I thinking when I signed up to make a dessert for the Bible study!"

As Ann Marie mapped out her return home after a long day on the job, the perpetual knot in the pit of her stomach tightened even harder as she worried, *How will I ever get it all done?* She was smart enough and seasoned enough to realize it was impossible for her to accomplish her present list of "Things to Do Today" in the amount of time she had available. In fact, if she had from lunchtime to bedtime, she still wouldn't have enough time.

Soberly, Ann Marie acknowledged that what needed to be done in the next ten hours was only the tip of the iceberg of responsibilities she lived with every day of her life. When she arrived home there would be dinner to fix, serve, and clean up, schoolwork for the kids (which was always a battle), baths and bedtimes to monitor, untold piles of laundry to wash (not to mention fold and put away), bills to pay (why was there never enough money?), cheap airfares to find for the family reunion this summer (if the rates were low enough), assisted-living facilities to research for her aging parents — and then

111

there was her husband, Bill, who always seemed to be in need of something . . . or everything!

THE BURDEN OF RESPONSIBILITY

Can you feel Ann Marie's pain? Her frustration? Her hopelessness? And can you relate to her quandary, her unhappiness? I can. Do you ever wake up in the morning and feel as though the weight of the world is on your shoulders . . . before you even get out of bed? Everyone seems to be looking to you for help. You wonder, *Just how many balls, plates, people, commitments, and responsibilities can I keep in the air at the same time?* The issue is not that you aren't responsible. It's just the opposite. You are *hyper*-conscious and aware of your many roles, duties, and responsibilities! That's why life seems to be such an impossible burden at times.

> *You are not alone. God is with you. And He gives you the power to make changes to ease your load.*

Well, if this is your concern — and I might add, your worry — then, congratulations! You are not alone! I want us to look at a Bible text right now that pretty much sums up how I've felt — and how I've acted — at times when my responsibilities seemed to be overwelming. Meet Martha, a woman who was preoccupied with the burden of her responsibilities.

PREOCCUPATION WITH RESPONSIBILITY

Can you imagine the stress you might feel if Jesus and His band of twelve were coming to your home for dinner . . . on top of everything else you had to do in a day's work? Martha's stress-out started as Jesus and His disciples arrived on her doorstep. Of course Martha, according to the custom of the day, welcomed everyone in for dinner! To compound Martha's work and hostessing problems, Mary, her sister, stopped helping her with the work and sat down when the Lord began to talk. As Martha spotted her at the feet of Jesus, she went into a tailspin. Why, Mary was listening to the Lord teach when she was supposed to be helping with the preparations!

Next we see how the pressure of responsibility affected Martha's relationships. Read about it in Luke 10.

But Martha was distracted with much serving, and she approached Him and said, "Lord, do You not care that my sister has left me to serve alone? Therefore tell her to help me" (verse 40).

How did Jesus respond to such an accusation and request? First, in His infinite wisdom He put His divine finger on the problem and then pointed Martha in a better direction — the right direction:

Martha, Martha, you are worried and troubled about many things. But one thing is needed, and Mary has chosen that good part, which will not be taken away from her (verses 41–42).

Quickly and precisely the Lord whittled Martha's life priorities down from the *many* to the *one*. In the words of one scholar, Jesus wanted Martha "to understand that because she was *worried and troubled about many things,* she was not making time for what was most important — *that good part."*[1]

THE DOWNSIDE OF RESPONSIBILITY

Married or single, you, like Martha — and me! — have mountains of responsibility. Responsibility in and of itself is not a bad thing. It's a good thing to experience the tension of having people to see, places to go, and things to do. This is what life is made of! It keeps us going, growing, active, alive, useful, involved, and alert. But there is also a downside, especially if we mishandle the burden of responsibility and act in ways that are not honoring to God or helpful to others. Unfortunately Martha succumbed and gave in to the downside of responsibility. She made her work her primary priority . . . instead of focusing on her worship. What was the fallout?

Martha became obsessed. Have you ever seen a woman who's so consummed with the task at hand that her face is hardened, furrowed, and drawn with anxiety? Why, she almost looks like she's in pain! Forget graciousness and sensitivity to others. This is the idea of the word "distracted" used to describe Martha's countenance as she tried to get Jesus to make her sister stop listening to Him and start lending her a hand with the preparations and serving. Martha was on a mission. She had a job to do. And nothing was going to stop her, including Jesus!

Martha became rude. Martha was so distraught with her tasks that she literally burst in upon Jesus and interrupted Him while He was teaching! Then in further frustration, she reproached Jesus for monopolizing

Mary's time, lashing out with a character accusation, "Lord, do You not care that my sister has left me to serve alone?" (Yes, Martha's pity party was in full swing!)

Martha became bossy. Pressure can easily get to us, causing us to act in a carnal, un-Christlike way. If you read the story of Jesus and the raising of Lazarus (Martha and Mary's brother) from the dead in John 11, you'll notice that Martha is a very respectful and reverent person at heart. But contrast this with the Martha we witness in our story in Luke 10. Here she is rude, abrupt, accusing, and harsh, even demanding the Lord to "tell her to help me"!

Martha's range of responses to her responsibilities is a perfect example — and a mirror — of how worry can destroy relationships and derail even the most noble projects and ministries. But, praise God, she had Someone who cared, understood, and loved her . . . no matter what — Someone who was able to redirect her focus.

JESUS UNDERSTANDS!

Martha is definitely out of control. But the Good Shepherd stops His teaching, turns to her, and calmly calls her by name . . . twice. Once might have shown impatience and irritation. But with the second use of her name, with the second "Martha," Jesus indicates He understands her frustration. You can almost hear His love for this dear woman and sense His understanding of her responsibilities and causes for worry. He says, "Martha, Martha, you are worried and troubled about many things" (verse 41). Doesn't that have a calming effect? It sure does for me!

Now, here's a thought for us. What issue at work, what household or family project, what ministry responsibility or challenge at home is causing you frustration? So much frustration, that you, like Martha, are obsessed, rude, and bossy? Take your worries to Jesus. He understands. Replace Martha's name with yours, and let Him say to you, "_____, _____, you are worried and troubled about many things." Then take Jesus' advice! Stop all your worrying and refocus on the "one thing" and the "good part." Sit down and rest at His feet. Let Him calm your heart and mind. Let Him teach you His ways. Let Him renew your perspective. Allow Jesus to remind you not to worry. Hear Him say to you . . .

Do not worry about your life, what you will eat or what you will drink; nor about your body, what you will put on (Matthew 6:25).

Why do you worry about clothing? (Matthew 6:28).

Do not worry, saying, "What shall we eat?" or "What shall we drink?" or "What shall we wear?" (Matthew 6:31).

Jesus' solution to your worries about your responsibilities centers on making two choices. First, focus on God, not on your work and responsibilities. In Martha's case, it was the business of fixing a meal and being a good hostess that distracted her from worshiping and enjoying her Lord. Mary, however, zoomed in on the one thing that really mattered. She focused on *Him.* She chose to sit at Jesus' feet to adore Him, listen to Him, and learn from Him. As Jesus noted, Mary chose "that good part," which could never be taken away from her (Luke 10:42).

> *Jesus is with you — loving you, taking care of you, guiding you, standing beside you, and calming your heart.*

The everyday responsibilities of life, your hectic schedule, and your endless to-do lists will always be a part of your day-in, day-out existence. And even though doing your duties and faithfully living out your roles are essential, in the larger scope of the Christian life they are not the most important things. What *is* vital is a closer walk with Jesus, growing in Him, and following Him with all your heart. Your relationship with Christ will remain throughout eternity. It and it alone is that which will not and cannot be taken away from you (verse 42). It is that which will sustain you in all your times of need.

Jesus spoke of this spiritual priority in the Sermon on the Mount when He said, "Your heavenly Father knows that you need all these things. But seek first the kingdom of God and His righteousness, and all these things shall be added to you" (Matthew 6:32–33). When God is your focus — your priority and the center of your minutes and days — you won't need to worry about your daily duties and circumstances . . . or anything else. Jesus will see you safely through your challenges. He will provide the wisdom you need to make right choices for handling them and the strength you need to endure them.

The second must-make choice is to focus on today. Teach yourself to take one day at a time. The last resort of a bona fide worrywart after all of today's worries are settled (or seem to be beyond hope) is to start worrying about *tomorrow's* possible problems. But just as Jesus instructs us not to worry about today, He also says we are not to be concerned about tomorrow, at least until tomorrow gets here! He says, therefore, that because God is your priority, "Do not worry about tomorrow, for tomorrow will worry about its own things. Sufficient for the day is its own trouble" (verse 34). And what about tomorrow? No worries! Jesus will be there too, to love you, take care of you, guide you, stay beside you, and calm your anxious heart!

Doing Your Part

Speaking of to-do lists, I've made one that will help both you and me do what's required of us in following God's plan for lasting peace of mind.

✓ *Remember the command.* Now what did Jesus say about worry? "Do *not* worry." This command — delivered in three clear, totally understandable words — should be enough to keep us from worrying, but, sad to say, it doesn't. As I wrote in the introduction to this book, worry is the result of a lack of hope and a lack of trust. Why would Jesus tell us not to worry? Does He know something we don't? Why, yes, He does! He knows the beginning from the end, and He knows how our dilemmas need to be handled. So obey His command. Do not worry! There is hope. Put your trust in Jesus. Turn your issues over to Him and trust Him to handle them for you or show you the best way to handle them.

I know you're probably thinking, "But you don't understand the burdens I'm forced to carry." Maybe I don't. But I do know that I too am constantly under the pile of my own burdens. I ask you, as I ask myself, how powerful is God? Don't you think that the God who created you and saved you and knows every detail there is to know about your problems will also see you through each and every trouble you're now facing or will ever face? We both know the answer, don't we? God will do His part. Be willing to do the part you must play in dealing with your issues. And what is your part? Trusting Him as you fulfill your responsibilities in your circumstances.

✓ *Revisit your priorities.* Jesus asked Martha to examine and reorder her priorities. Mary had already chosen worshiping Jesus as her first priority. Martha, on the other hand, chose serving instead of stopping and sitting at Jesus' feet to adore Him and take in His word. True, she was serving the Lord but, as Jesus pointed out, that was not to be her chief priority. Service is fine, noble, worthy, and necessary. But when it gets in the way of your relationship with Christ, it's counterproductive.

✓ *Re-examine your service.* Have you ever heard of Pareto's law, also known as the 80/20 rule? This law states that, for many events, roughly 80 percent of the effects come from 20 percent of the causes. When applied to the church, it implies that 80 percent of the work of service is generally done by 20 percent of the people. I'm guessing you are one of the few doing the work of and for the many. When you look around, you can't help but notice all that needs to be done. So you step in to help and end up doing more than you planned on or should be doing. You wake up one day trying to do things in areas way outside your spiritual giftedness. All of this adds up to extra burdens, pressures, and worries that weren't yours to carry.

Take a fresh, long-overdue look at all your areas of service in the church. Which ones could be delegated or deleted? (The same applies at home. What work chores can you give your children to do?) Ask other people to help you determine your areas of greatest contribution. Then ask to be relieved of the rest. If you're married, sit down with your husband and ask for his advice and insights about which ministries he thinks you should keep and which ones you should drop. Above all, as you examine your service, don't neglect to evaluate your relationship with God and your relationship with your family. They take priority over your service to others. Serve them first. Then serve others.

✓ *Revise your schedule.* Once you determine your areas of greatest priority, map out a schedule that reflects those priorities and allows for an orderly life. If you're stressed, worried, and overly committed, your life will lack order. With a few revisions on your part, you can enjoy an ordered life, a Spirit-filled life free from stress and worry.

✓ *Reap the blessings.* If your life is ordered, prioritized, and Spirit-filled, you will have love, joy, peace, and patience. You'll be kind, always seeking to do good things for others, and faithful, gentle, and self-controlled. Possessing these qualities will mean you have gained the secret of being able to follow Jesus' command not to worry. As you walk and live by the Spirit, yours will be a blessed life and a blessing to others.

Breaking the Worry Habit . . . Forever!

After talking to so many women who love the Lord and want to serve Him with all their heart, soul, mind, and strength, I'm guessing that you too take your responsibilities seriously. Maybe so much so that you worry about how you're going to manage all the responsibilities and relationships that are on your plate at home *and* fulfill everything you've committed yourself to outside the home. But is it possible that you're trying to do more than God is asking of you? Or maybe the reason you're so busy is that you're taking on responsibilities that aren't yours? Maybe you're volunteering too often or for too much?

Here's a thought. What if there are just a few things God is asking of you? Just a few things that are required of you? A few things that demand your faithfulness? Well, that's the truth. God has a unique list of responsibilities that are just for you. (For starters, look at the list in Titus 2:3–5.) Ask Him to help you write out your list based on His list. Then ask Him to infuse you with His wisdom and empower you with His strength to faithfully carry out your list.

And here's another thought. God isn't asking you to fulfill your present responsibilities forever. Some duties will need to be done every day you're alive. Others, however, will come and go with the seasons of your life. You need to focus your attention, time, and energies only on the tasks God has for you today. Then tomorrow ask Him what His priorities are for your life. They may or may not be the same as today's. And tomorrow ask Him once again to equip you. This is how you break the worry habit . . . forever

— by looking at each day's true priorities and then looking fully into God's face and moving forward in His power and grace! Like Mary, choose the one thing and live out His will. When pressure mounts, follow Mary's path to peace.

- ✄ *Stop what you're doing* — all your busyness, all your stewing, all your doing, all your running around in circles, all your accusing and complaining.

- ✄ *Sit down* — both in body and in heart.

- ✄ *Seek God's peace and priorities* — through prayer.

- ✄ *Start up again* — with a quiet heart, the right attitude, and God's right direction for your efforts.

You will keep him in perfect peace whose mind is stayed on You.
ISAIAH 26:3

7

BE CAREFUL WITH THAT!

*Do not lay up for yourselves treasures
on earth . . .
but lay up for yourselves treasures in heaven.*
MATTHEW 6:19–20

Finally Sue had the home of her dreams! She and Robert had been buying and fixing up old homes ever since they had married. Each home usually took about two years of residence before the "fixer upper" was ready to sell again. They had purchased, remodeled, and sold homes all over the city. Wherever there was a bargain that could be turned into a profit, Sue and Robert were right there with a down payment. As profitable as it was, though, there had been a personal price to pay. Their kids had grown up without roots. Wherever they lived wasn't really "home" — it was just the next house that needed to be fixed up for selling. Sue had lost count of the number of school districts the kids had been students in.

But things were going to be different now. With their hard-earned profits, Sue and Robert were reaching the goal they had set 20 years ago. They had at last bought a home in one of the best neighborhoods in town. And the home was only two years old and wouldn't need anything done to it for a long time. Whew! Sue could sit back and enjoy her new home for a change. But that was just the problem. She couldn't! Worry and anxiety moved right into her new home! Every spill, every scratch, every act of normal usage drove her crazy with worry and impulsive tidiness. To make matters worse, her obsession made Robert and the kids as miserable as she was. No one could relax. How, Sue wondered, could something so good become such a nightmare?

A PERSONAL CONFESSION

Can you identify in any way with Sue? I

sure can. When Jim and I married, we wanted many of the same things Sue and most everyone else wants. We wanted good jobs, a good income, a new car, and an exciting lifestyle — with, of course, the funds to finance it. As time went by and we obtained these goals, we began to wish for a terrific home to own, decorate, and fill with brand-new designer furniture. Within eight years of marriage, we had all this. And because Jim received many raises and promotions and bonuses, we had a stock portfolio and a large savings account. Life was good.

With joy-filled hearts we gladly stepped into a new life where there weren't any voids.

But then what? There we were, stuffing our lives full of stuff, and still we were restless. So we traveled. We camped. We took night classes. We joined a sailing club. We developed hobbies like photography, bicycling, and woodworking. We regularly read every book published that made the *New York Times* "Top Ten Bestseller List." We played chess and belonged to a competitive bridge club.

Still we couldn't shake the emptiness. As hard as we tried, and as much money as we earned and spent, and as many things as we stockpiled and owned, we still searched for something more. But nothing lasted and nothing satisfied . . . and we weren't even 30 years old.

Well, praise God for His intervention in our lives. By His grace I heard and responded to the gospel message of salvation through Jesus Christ, and Jim renewed his commitment to Christ. With joy-filled hearts we gladly stepped into a new life, a life where there are never any voids — a life filled with Jesus Christ and goals centered around eternity and eternal values.

It wasn't long before Jim resigned from his job to go back to school to prepare for ministry. We sold our home and most of the furniture and moved into a very small and much older home that had nothing but the basics. Later in life our financial situation did stabilize, but our perspective on our possessions was permanently altered.

PUTTING POSSESSIONS INTO A PROPER PERSPECTIVE

Now back to Sue. Ambition and industry are excellent attributes. And providing income and a home were great goals which required commitment, dedication, and a lot of elbow grease. They weren't easy or glamourous goals Sue and her husband set, but they desired to better their financial status for the family's sake. They were also willing to do a lot of hard work and use their skills to get ahead. The problem for Sue came at the end of her process when the family at last moved into her dream home. It was then that her "possession" — her house — began to skew her perspective on what was really important. You see, the home wasn't *her* possession. She was *its* possession! In the words of Albert Schweitzer, a doctor who spent much of his life practicing medicine in Africa, "If you have something you cannot give up, you don't own it, it owns you."

The word "possession" means something owned, occupied, or controlled. But in Sue's case, her possession became something that controlled her. The issue for you and me is not whether we own something. It's whether we can let go of it. Maybe these thoughts on how you and I should view our possessions will help.

Possessions can divide your allegiance to God. We live in a materialistic society. All you have to do to know this is true is look at people's garages! People generally have incredibly wonderful two-car (or more) garages, but they still park their cars in the driveway or on the street. Why? Because of all the "stuff" that's piled to the ceiling in their garages.

Jesus knew possessions could become a major spiritual problem. He is the one who said, "No one can serve two masters. Either he will hate the one and love the other, or he will be devoted to the one and despise the other. You cannot serve both God and Money" (Matthew 6:24 NIV).

Take a moment to think about and evaluate your attitude toward your possessions. Do you own any "things" that you couldn't immediately walk away from? Remember, Dr. Schweitzer said, "If you have something you cannot give up, you don't own it, it owns you." Now take another moment to read the story of the rich young ruler in Matthew 19:16-24. This young man wanted to follow Jesus. However, the first thing Jesus asked him to do in following Him was to "go sell what you have and give to the poor" (verse 21). The man's response? "He went away sorrowful, for he had great possessions" (verse 22). This man needed an attitude adjustment toward his wealth and possessions in relation to his service to the Lord and to others. Do you?

Possessions don't last. Do you remember when your car was brand-new and shiny . . . and now it's riddled with dents, dings, and permanently imbedded dirt? Or the fabulous new outfit you got for a special occasion . . . and now it's hopelessly outdated? Jesus zooms in with a reality check. He's got a command for us and a reason for it.

Do not lay up for yourselves treasures on earth, where moth and rust destroy and where thieves break in and steal (Matthew 6:19).

Because of the temporary nature of our possessions, Jesus tells us exactly where we should place our focus, and again He tells us why.

But lay up for yourselves treasures in heaven, where neither moth nor rust destroys and where thieves do not break in and steal. For where your treasure is, there your heart will be also (verses 20–21).

Where is your focus? Where is your "treasure"? Put another way, what occupies your thoughts and time? The goal is to make sure your first loyalties — your priority heart commitments — are on the right things, the things that cannot fade away, the things that can never be stolen, the things that cannot wear out (and are never out of fashion!). In short, the things that last — the things that are eternal.

Possessions are a stewardship. You and I have what we have by the grace of God, right down to "give us this day our daily bread" (Matthew 6:11). If we have the attitude that we're here on earth to take care of the Lord's possessions, His treasure, and His property, we'll be less enamored by materialism and less devoted to amassing possessions. God is the owner of everything we have. We are merely His caretakers of what He gives us. The only concern we should have about possessions is making sure we're good stewards of God's goods!

That's what Jesus was saying in the parable of the three servants in Matthew 25:14–30. Before their master left on a trip, each servant was given an amount of money "according to his own ability" (verse 15). The master returned and asked each man to give an accounting of his use of the money. The issue wasn't the *amount* of money each was given — that was determined by the master. The issue was the *attitude* toward the master's money — that was determined by the individual. The master was interested in how faithful each servant had been with what he had given him. Only one of the servants was condemned for his selfish focus and disregard for what belonged to someone else. We become poor stewards of God's possessions if we think only of ourselves and fail to think of our Master.

Possessions do not equal contentment. They may even have the opposite effect. Take a look around you. Do most people seem to have an abundance? Now look again and ask, how many of these people are content? Jesus told a story about a rich

> *Only as we focus on Christ and relegate our money and possessions to stewardship status will we be content.*

landowner whose barns were utterly filled up with grain. But was he content? Obviously not, because he thought about his predicament and decided, "I will pull down my barns and build greater, and there I will store all my crops and my goods" (Luke 12:18).

The words I love best when it comes to

contentment are these:

Now godliness with contentment is great gain. For we brought nothing into this world, and it is certain we can carry nothing out. And having food and clothing, with these we shall be content (1 Timothy 6:6–8).

These are facts, truths, and an exhortation. But this message goes on to include a warning:

But those who desire to be rich fall into temptation and a snare, and into many foolish and harmful lusts which drown men in destruction and perdition. For the love of money is a root of all kinds of evil, for which some have strayed from the faith in their greediness, and pierced themselves through with many sorrows (verses 9–10).

Only as we focus on Christ and not on our money and our stuff will we be content. When our eyes and hearts are not fixed on Him, we succumb to temptation and lust after what is foolish and harmful. It's good to remember that loving money and possessions leads to all kinds of evil. Search your heart once again. Where is your focus? On

Jesus, or on jewelry? On the Master, or on money? On the Person of Christ, or on possessions? On your heavenly Father, or on your home? On worshiping God, or on Wall Street? On Jesus, the only thing that matters, or on everything else?

Possessions are not the end goal. People worry about their things because acquiring them is generally seen as a major goal in life. We worry about not having them. Then we worry about how to get them. Then once we have them, we, like Sue, worry about keeping and maintaining them — about scratches, spills, wear and tear, breakage, damage, fire, theft, a sinking stock market, loss, and any and everything else that might separate us from our money and belongings. No, having more does not bring contentment. The truth is, the more we have, the more we have to worry about.

So what's the solution? Understand that possessions are not to be hoarded — that's greed. And possessions are not to be guarded — that's a burden. They are to be shared and given away — that's a blessing. Possessions held lightly become opportunities to serve God and people. Sharing God's blessings with others is the true goal. The end goal of having is giving.

Possessions do not satisfy. People believe that any emptiness they feel in life can be filled with things. But only Jesus can fill every void in our souls. Think about Solomon, the richest man in the world during his lifetime. After he had every imaginable thing he could possibly possess, all he could say was that "indeed all was vanity and grasping for the wind. There was no profit under the sun" (Ecclesiastes 2:11). The reality is, the more you have the more you want.

After all this, do you understand exactly what the usefulness of money and possessions is? It's to bless others! To help others. To better others. To support others. If God has blessed you and your family with finances and possessions, you need to take every opportunity to share with others. A house is to be used for hospitality. A car is to be used to take a senior citizen to the doctor or to church or shopping. Food in the refrigerator is to be prepared for a family who has a new baby or someone who has had surgery or requires special meals after a cancer treatment.

HOLDING YOUR POSSESSIONS LIGHTLY

If you have the attitude that you're taking care of the Lord's property, the Lord's money, and the Lord's goods, you'll be more willing to make what you have available to others. You'll be less worried about what you can keep and more focused on what you can give away. Many of God's people in the Bible gave generously.

Former slaves gave sacrificially. The children of Israel left Egypt after 400 years of bondage and poverty. They left with the clothes on their backs, what they could carry, and the gold, silver, and clothing their masters had given them. It is amazing that even after life-long poverty, they held onto their newfound wealth lightly and responded generously to the call to provide materials to furnish the Tabernacle being built for worshiping God. They not only gave, but they gave so much that they were finally restrained from giving any more (Exodus 35:20–36:7).

A widow gave all her food. During a severe drought, the prophet Elijah was sent to a widow who was gathering a few sticks to prepare the last of her food for herself and her son. After they ate their final meal, she and her son planned to die of starvation. There was no more food. But when Elijah asked for the food she was preparing, she willingly gave it all to him! In response to her obedience, God provided oil and flour for her, her son, and Elijah for many days until it rained and crops began to appear again (1 Kings 17:8–16).

A widow gave all her money. Jesus made an observation as the people came giving money to the temple treasury. The rich people gave according to their riches. However a lone widow gave her last two pieces of money. Everything she had! Of her heart and sacrifice, the Lord said, "This poor widow has put in more than all those who have given to the treasury; for they all put in out of their abundance, but she out of her poverty put in all that she had, her whole livelihood" (Mark 12:43–44). Many gave some, but one gave all.

A disciple gave all his property. As the early church began to grow, there were great financial needs for the widows and others who chose to remain in Jerusalem after the Feast of Pentecost. It was then that many — including Barnabas — "who were possessors of lands or houses sold them, and brought the proceeds of the things that were sold, and laid them at the apostles' feet" (Acts 4:32–37). Barnabas later became a trusted associate to Paul.

This is quite a convicting roll call, isn't it? I'm not suggesting that you sell all or give all. But what I am recommending is that you hold your possessions lightly. Pry your fingers off each and every one of your goods, your properties, your financial holdings, and your bank accounts. Then with a heart of love, be willing to give. That's the attitude God is looking for — a willing, caring, generous, unselfish, trusting heart.

Doing Your Part

God has done His part. He has given you the ultimate possession — eternal life in His Son. And He has given you the Holy Spirit as His guarantee of that eternal life (2 Corinthians 1:22). And Jesus has gone to prepare a place for you and will come again for you (John 14:1–3). All of God's provision should take care of any worries you are having about your earthly possessions, which diminish to nothing when compared with the incomparable value of spending eternity with God! So now, while you're waiting for heaven, it's up to you to do your part in breaking your worry habit about money and possessions. Start now — today!

✓ *Embrace a heavenly perspective.* You are only on this earth for a short time, so enjoy your family and whatever possessions God blesses you with. But that's as far as it goes. You can't take your car or your house or your jewelry with you when you leave this earth. No, they will be left behind. So why not let them go now . . . at least in your heart and mind? Then you can enjoy the rest of your life without worrying about your possessions.

✓ *Evaluate what you have.* Are you like the bride who received four toasters? Most of what you have is excess. How many cars, TVs, outfits, or shoes — or toasters! — do you really need? Maybe it's time to look at what you have and ask yourself, "Do I really need all of this?" If you're like most people, your answer will probably be a resounding *no!* This is a good first step. And the second step?

✓ *Enumerate what you are willing to give away.* This is the next step of rehabilitation from all the laying up of treasure you're doing on earth. You've already admitted you can do without some things, so let the getting-rid-of-it process begin. Start cleaning out and giving away the excess. Bless someone else with your abundance. Or have a yard sale, garage sale, tag sale. Then take that money and use it for God or for His people, or save it for later for some worthy need in your family — education for your children, supporting aging parents, quitting your job, and the like.

✓ *Examine what you want.* There's a difference between "wants" and "needs." Jesus promised He will take care of all your needs (Matthew 6:31–32). Unfortunately, if you're like most people, you've added, " . . . and I'll take care of my wants." Make it a rule not to buy anything on an impulse. Wait! This is where prayer comes in. Start praying about each and every purchase. Pray until there is a peace that this desired item is truly necessary for your health and welfare or that it will in some way enrich your family.

✓ *Enjoy freedom from worry.* And let me add "peace" as well. Materialism is the curse of our affluent society, and

Christians are as guilty as anyone else in their neighborhoods. But when you gain an eternal perspective and do your part, you will gain great freedom from worrying about possessions.

Breaking the Worry Habit . . . Forever!

It's been said "attitude is everything." When it comes to habits, attitude truly is everything. We put up with or condone or justify our habits, which are mostly bad ones, because we've told ourselves they're okay, or at least they're not so bad. But let's do a reality check. Try labeling the habit of worrying as "sin." As I said in the introduction to this book, worry — any worry! — is a sin that denies the power of God. It's a sin that fails to trust God. It's a sin that fails to believe God. And it's a sin that fails to love God. So take these few serious steps to help you break any and all worry habits about any and all things, including your possessions:

> *Step 1:* Label worry as sin.
> *Step 2:* Confess your worries about your possessions as sin.
> *Step 3:* Acknowledge God's desire and

ability to provide all your needs.

Step 4: Obediently follow the many commands in Scripture that tell you not to worry or be anxious.

Again, I'm not a student of the Greek language, but my husband, who is, tells me that the many commands we've been addressing in this book are actually exhorting us to stop constantly worrying about even one thing. We are to literally worry about *nothing.* These commands are in the Bible because God recognizes the habitual tendency of the human heart to worry about the problems and difficulties of life. Therefore God tells us exactly what to do: He says to stop continuing the habit of worry. It's that simple!

Now . . . what was that problem?

Because the LORD is my Shepherd,
I have everything I need!
PSALM 23:1 TLB

8
I Don't Want to Go!

*But when he saw that the wind
was boisterous, he was afraid.*
MATTHEW 14:30

Rita had been a cautious person all her life.
Even as a child she seldom — no, make that
never — took chances. She couldn't help but
worry about what might happen if she flew
in an airplane, or got too close to the window in a skyscraper, or traveled too far from
land in a boat. And then there was that vacation when her family wanted to get a picture
of everyone standing next to the rail at the

edge of the Grand Canyon for their annual Christmas card. The very thought of being that close to the edge (never mind there was a rail) caused her to hyperventilate . . . which, of course, ruined their chances for a photo and almost ruined their vacation! Her husband, Alan, almost had to call the paramedics to give her something to calm her down.

And don't get Rita started on the weather! She was thrilled when she married Alan and he was transferred out of "tornado alley" in the Midwest. The newlyweds ended up in sunny Southern California, where tornados were practically unheard of. But one month after their move, surprise! Rita experienced a 6.7 earthquake that almost destroyed their new home, not to mention the hundreds of aftershocks and the damage they did to her home . . . and nerves! It took Rita and Alan almost a year to get their lives back in order after that . . . and, well, she never got over it. From that day on, Rita woke up and went to bed worrying about earthquakes.

Finally after months of Rita's pleading, whining, crying, and visiting the doctor often for stronger medications, Alan gave in and was given a transfer to New Orleans — just six months before Hurricane Katrina slammed the coast of Louisiana and almost wiped New Orleans off the map.

Worrying About the "What Ifs"

You might be reading this and telling yourself, *No way am I as bad as Rita!* when it comes to fretting about life and its many circumstances. But if it's not a fear of heights, flying, earthquakes, or hurricanes, your specialty may be worrying about global warming, or a flood, or, as my daughter just experienced, a tsunami warning. Or maybe your worries run in the vein of the possibility of catching some rare disease from germs off a handrail you touched. Maybe you are contemplating wearing a surgical mask to keep you safe from swine flu. Or maybe your worries extend to fires (we've had one . . . and it changes your thinking!), mudslides, avalanches, and, well, anything nature can throw at you.

Whatever circumstance — or potential circumstance — causes you to worry, in most cases it's something you can do very little, if anything, about. (Does this sound familiar?) Oh, you can head for the cellar when a tornado is sighted, as I did often while growing up in Oklahoma. Or you can travel inland like my daughter did — twice — when a hurricane is about to slam into your area of the coast. But what about earthquakes? Our family survived two large ones (6.6 and 6.8 on the Richter scale) while living in Southern

California, and those were only the biggies! What about random acts of violence? Or a break-in? Our home has been robbed, and our car has been broken into. Or the possibility of a car wreck? My aunt was killed in a car accident in West Texas where you can drive for miles without seeing another car. I'm sure you have your own list of worry topics. And both of our lists could go on and on!

This was exactly the problem poor Rita was having. Her endless list had consumed her thoughts, disrupted her productivity, severely strained her marriage, and even jeopardized her husband's job more than once! Her fretting was possibly the cause of the new physical problems she was experiencing. And more seriously, her many fears and anxieties were undermining everything she was trying to teach her children about faith and trust in God.

"WHERE IS YOUR FAITH?"

Faith — or lack of it — is precisely the point Jesus was making to His disciples, and the exact question He asked them during a storm on the Sea of Galilee. Read it for yourself:

Now it happened, on a certain day, that He [Jesus] got into a boat with His disciples.

And He said to them, "Let us cross over to the other side of the lake." And they launched out. But as they sailed He fell asleep. And a windstorm came down on the lake, and they were filling with water, and were in jeopardy. And they came to Him and awoke Him, saying, "Master, Master, we are perishing!" Then He arose and rebuked the wind and the raging of the water. And they ceased, and there was a calm. But He said to them, "Where is your faith?" (Luke 8:22–25).

There is a difference between worry and concern. Concern moves you to prayer, action, and preparation, but worry immobilizes you. That seems to be what was happening with the disciples. As expert fishermen who were familiar with the Sea of Galilee and its occasional stormy conditions, they could at least have tried to bail the water out of the rapidly filling boat! But instead, out of worry and fear, they came to Jesus for help. This is still early in their relationship with Him, so the disciples didn't yet fully grasp who Jesus was. And even after He calmed the storm, they said to one another, "Who can this be? For He commands even the winds and water, and they obey Him!" (verse 25).

For you and me, the bottom line with

worry and real fear is the same as it was for the disciples — asking and answering the question, "Where is your faith?"

FAITH FIGHTS FEAR AND WORRY

When we consider Jesus' question, "Where is your faith?" we are not talking about *the* faith, as used to refer to belief in a set of doctrinal truths that represent Christianity. The faith we are considering involves trust. Worry is a lack of trust. Worry says, "My problems and issues are too big for even God to deal with." Trust says, "I can do all things through Christ who strengthens me" (Philippians 4:13).

Wouldn't life be more pleasant, more enjoyable, if you and I could strengthen our faith and trust in the Lord? The answer is, absolutely! So what does trust look like? And what marks a woman of strong faith?

Trust exhibits courage. Trapped between the Red Sea and the oncoming army of Pharaoh, the fleeing Israelites melted in despair. They were in total panic and fearful for their lives. They would have run from their enemy if there had been any place to go. So they started whining and complaining and murmuring and blaming Moses, the leader God personally appointed, for what was about to happen. But what did Moses say to them? "Do not be afraid. Stand still, and see the salvation of the LORD, which He will accomplish for you today . . . The LORD will fight for you" (Exodus 14:13–14). And that's exactly what happened. The Red Sea miraculously opened, the Israelites walked through the Red Sea on dry ground to safety, and the Egyptian army was totally destroyed when the waters returned to normal. So what's the lesson for us?

> *Trust holds fast, standing firm until deliverance arrives or a solution is found.*

Worry and fear see no hope. Like the disciples who focused on the water, the waves, and their sinking boat instead of their Savior, the Israelites fixated on the strength of their enemy instead of the strength of their Almighty God to take care of and deliver His people. They became cowards, ready to stop following God's plan and flee from adversity. Worry and fear caused them to believe all was lost.

Trust, on the other hand, sees nothing but hope. Trust is courageous and holds firm until deliverance arrives or a solution is found. Trust believes all is not lost and never will be in God's economy. Trust courageously waits for God's grace and help.

Trust manifests confidence. Normally we don't lean against anything like a wall or pillar unless we're confident the object will bear our weight, right? And when it comes to our problems, we don't normally ask for help unless we're confident a friend or counselor or pastor can help, right? Trust gives us the confidence to accept someone's help, or it gives us the assurance that the action we're about to take is the right path or will turn out okay. Because we have trust in someone or something, we can make more confident decisions.

Think again about the story of the disciples and the storm on the Sea of Galilee. There was another occasion when the disciples were in a similar stormy condition on the same sea. In this instance, Jesus was not with them. However, as the storm increased, the disciples saw Jesus walking toward them on the water. Suddenly they were not only fearful of the storm but also of what they thought was a ghost (Matthew 14:25–26).

Then Jesus spoke to them and said, "Be of good cheer! It is I; do not be afraid" (verse 27). With the confidence that came from knowing it was Jesus and not a ghost, Peter

153

believed that, if Jesus asked him to get out of the boat and come to Him, he too could walk on the water. "So He [Jesus] said, 'Come.'" With the confidence that's derived only from fully trusting in Jesus, Peter stepped out of the boat and, miracle of miracles, he "walked on the water to go to Jesus" (verse 29).

Unfortunately, Peter soon took his focus off Jesus and zoomed in on the wind and the waves. As he began sinking into the water, Jesus caught him and they both got into the boat. Peter's confidence had turned into doubt, as Jesus pointed out when He asked, "O you of little faith, why did you doubt?" (verse 31). And, dear friend, our confidence, like Peter's, is only as strong as our trust in Jesus' ability and promises to see us through any and all trials, circumstances, and disasters.

Trust demonstrates belief. One of the earliest — and key — verses dealing with the importance of trust in God is Genesis 15:5–6. Here God gives the childless Abraham a promise to make of him a great nation with descendants as numerous as the stars (verse 5). Abraham had nothing to base the fulfillment of this promise upon. Everything in his life was pointing in the opposite direction.

He was about 85 years old. And Sarah, his wife, was past childbearing age. So what did Abraham do? "He believed in the LORD" (verse 6). Abraham put his trust in God's word to him, in the promises God had made to him. And Abraham's trust was rewarded by salvation. Verse 6 continues, saying God accounted it to Abraham for righteousness.[1]

In Abraham's case — and ours as well — trusting means believing. It means putting our confidence or belief in Christ to forgive our sins, to make us right with God, and to empower us to live for Him. All of this means we fight fear and worry with a rock-solid trust in Jesus to see us through any and all circumstances.

Trust models patience. We live in a "quick fix" world. "I want what I want . . . and I want it now!" is our slogan. Even when it comes to trusting God, we can wait a few hours or a few days, but don't ask us to wait too long! How well would your trust hold up if you had to wait for 25 years for something? That's how long Abraham had to wait for the fulfillment of God's promise to give him an heir and to make a great nation of his descendants. God's first promise to Abraham was made to him when he was 75 years old. And the fulfillment came at age 100 — 25 years later! How long could you wait?

Trusting God is difficult when nothing seems to be happening, when everything seems to be in slow motion, or when everything *wrong* seems to be happening! But trust is unshakable. No matter what might be happening around us, we trust in God's ability to see us through our life conditions.

A word of caution: Impatience also makes us want to take matters into our own hands. That's what Sarah did in Genesis 16:1–6. She created her own solution to their problem. And the consequences and ramifications of her meddling are still rocking world peace today. Please resist the temptation to think God has forgotten you. And equally resist the temptation to come up with your own plans and solutions to your situation. Have patience. Trust God. Wait for Him to act, even if it takes 25 years . . . or more!

Trust displays obedience. Trust is always the harder road. The road less traveled. The road that demands obedience and the possibility of a sacrifice. Fast-forward in Abraham's story. Abraham steadfastly believed in God's promise of offspring. And he patiently waited on God's timing for 25 years. At last he had his heir, his son Isaac. But God was not through testing and strengthening Abraham's trust in Him. God asked Abraham to sacrifice his only son! Abraham's immediate response? Obedience (Genesis 22:3). Abraham was given the order to kill his son one day, and on the next he set out to comply. But this was only a test, and God did not require that Abraham sacrifice his son (verse 12).

Jesus put such trust this way: "If you love Me, keep My commandments" (John 14:15). In other words, "If you love Me, trust Me. Obey Me!" Obedience is a hard pill to swallow for most people — even Christians! And what makes this so remarkable is that Christians have already demonstrated trust by the greatest of all acts — putting their eternal destiny into the hands of God. So what's the big deal when it comes to worry? All we have to do is follow Jesus commands, obey, and refuse to worry!

Doing Your Part

We live in a world filled with danger. Just look out your window. It's easy to succumb to worry, as poor Rita did. We now know God's solution for all of the fears we Ritas give in to. He wants us to trust Him.

Trust. Trust in the Lord. We hear of trust

and read of it daily in the Bible. Just the sound and thought of trust makes us yearn for it in greater measure. So how do we strengthen this essential element of our spiritual walk? How do we grow to the point where we don't waver the next time a perceived threat appears on the horizon? How do we gain the peace of mind a solid trust in God brings to our hearts? Here are two things you can do.

✓ *Build a close relationship with Christ.* A relationship with Jesus Christ starts with salvation. But it can and must be cultivated from that point on so it's fresh, strong, and powerful on a day-by-day basis. It is this vibrant friendship with your Lord that will sustain you in times and situations when you might be prone to worry or be fearful. This moment-by-moment connection is referred to as "walking in the Spirit." It doesn't happen naturally or automatically. If that were true, Paul would have no need to give us a *command* to "walk in the Spirit" (Galatians 5:16). So, as you stay close to Jesus, His Spirit — the Holy Spirit — will help you not to give in to fleshly responses like worry, fear, dread, panic, and anxiety.

How can you stay close to Jesus?

- *Read God's Word.* We trust those we know to be trustworthy. The primary place to learn of Jesus' power to take care of His people and His faithfulness in doing so is in the Bible. When I was a new Christian, my mentor had me read through the four Gospels (Matthew, Mark, Luke, and John) four times every year. If you think that sounds like a lot of reading and time, it's not. It's one chapter — only *one chapter!* — a day. It takes only about two or three minutes to touch the Savior's life each day, to walk with Him, to learn about Him, to see how He interacted with people, to observe His character, and to witness His relationship with God the Father. Believe me, it will be the best two minutes of your day.

- *Pray for His guidance.* Each day I approach prayer with the apostle Paul in mind. He asked the Lord, "Lord, what do You want me to do?" (Acts 9:6). This is a simple way of asking God for guidance. Whatever you're involved in or facing, whatever is happening to you at any single minute, whatever surprise or tragedy appears out of nowhere, pray immediately, "Lord, what do You want me to do?" Even a split-second pause to ask God for His counsel about your situation will help give you direction. This is one way you can

> *Trust begins at salvation, but it must also be developed through daily use.*

tap into God's wisdom anywhere, anytime, no matter what's going on. James wrote, "If any of you lacks wisdom, let him ask of God . . . and it will be given to him" (James 1:5).

And here's another thought regarding the act of prayer. You cannot be talking to God and be anxious at the same time. The mere act of deciding to talk to God, involve God, and turn your thoughts toward Him takes your eye and emotions off what's in front of you, diluting its consuming power over you. Every heartfelt word or thought of prayer increases your trust in Him. Why wouldn't it? You're communicating with the most powerful Person in the world and in the universe, not to mention the Person who loves you completely and has promised to care for and protect you all the days of your life.

As you strengthen your walk with Jesus — and you learn more about Him in His Word and remember to talk things over with Him — His power infuses you through His Spirit. The result? You can resist all sorts of temptations, including the temptation to fret or worry about your circumstances. Why worry . . . when you can trust in the Lord with all your heart?

✓ *Build up your trust in Christ.* If a muscle isn't used, it withers and becomes useless. But if that same muscle is exercised and developed, it grows strong and powerful. Trust is the same way. Trust begins at salvation but must be developed through daily use. This occurs every time you turn your life issues over to Jesus and allow Him to lead. When you try to do things on your own, your "trust muscle" isn't used, and in time it becomes weak. Then, because your faith — or trust — is weak, you do and say things that you know you shouldn't. Or when something trying comes your way, you panic because you don't know what to do or how to handle it because it's been so long since you put your trust muscle to use.

At last, hopefully, there comes a point when you are backed into a corner and there seem to be no options, and you finally turn to God. It is then that your trust muscle is re-engaged, reactivated. The sad thing is that trust should have been your first reaction to any issue! When you are in the habit of using your trust muscle, it becomes your almost automatic response. The muscle awaits your beck and call, ready, willing, and able to see you through.

The life of Peter demonstrates how trust can be weak and atrophied or strong and well-developed. First, a negative example. Just after Jesus was taken into custody by the Jewish leaders the night before His crucifixion, Peter followed behind and ended up sitting by a fire where he was identified and confronted as one of Jesus' disciples. Peter failed to stand with Jesus and denied he even knew the Lord (Mark 14:66–71).

This lapse of trust is a sad page in the life of Peter. But later his lack of trust and courage was reversed as he stood before the great religious council. There he was threatened and told not to speak of Jesus. Yet Peter boldly, in a full-of-faith manner, responded, "We ought to obey God rather than men" (Acts 5:29). Peter's trust had grown, so much so that he was ready to take on the world for Jesus' sake! In fact, he helped turn the world upside down for Christ!

Breaking the Worry Habit . . . Forever!

As you read about Peter's up-and-down struggles, are you looking into a mirror? You and I can and must strive to develop a greater trust in God for even the smallest areas of need or concern. Then, when truly big issues arise, our faith and trust are of such strength and magnitude that we are able to move forward and gain the victory.

Every morning you wake up to a fresh new day. And every day you receive a new chance to make it a day of trusting God with anything and everything that comes your way. So, if you're like me and don't even need an alarm clock because you automatically wake up worrying about something, tell yourself what I tell myself —

Stop it! Stop worrying! As I've said throughout this book, worry is natural. Worry is easy. Worry is a habit. But you and I are looking for the *super*natural. So we put the skids on worry and stop it and look up instead. Then —

Start praying! Turn your thoughts upward. Purposefully begin thinking about God. Take your worries and problems and sorrow and grief and anger and fear immediately to Him. You can even begin your prayer with scripture. Pray:

Lord, Your Word says I'm to trust in the Lord with all my heart. So Lord, I'm turning to you. I'm choosing to take my eyes off my troubles and to look to You instead. I admit my tendency to worry, and I hate it! It's a blatant act of failing to trust You, Your control over my life, and Your love for me. Help me to strengthen my faith in You. Help me to trust You completely. Lord, here's my problem. What do You want me to do?

Step out in faith! Exercise that trust muscle. Get moving. Do whatever God communicates to you. Do whatever you can to manage your fear-and-anxiety-producing problem. And trust God. Trust Him for wisdom regarding your issue. Trust Him for love for the people involved in your issue. Trust Him for a sound mind in dealing with your issue. And trust Him for power as you remain steadfast and keep trusting in Him.

And one last word. You may have to do this minute by minute, and certainly problem by problem. But your goal is to break your worry habit and build your trust habit. Just for today — refuse to worry, do your part, and turn to God and trust Him.

God has not given us a spirit of fear,
but of power and of love and
of a sound mind.
2 TIMOTHY 1:7

9
What Goes Around Comes Around

Honor your father and your mother.
EXODUS 20:12

Finally! Betty had made it. She had arrived! Things were good between her and her husband. The kids were grown and married with grandbabies coming on a regular basis, and she had just been promoted to a very exciting position at work. Oh, there would be much more work and responsibility, but the pay and increased benefits would make all the extra effort worth it! Yes, things seemed to finally be going Betty's way. And then the phone rang . . .

Betty had worked late the night before. She'd had only a few hours of sleep and was running late as she got ready for work. She was running so late she almost didn't answer the phone . . . until she saw the readout on the phone. It was her parents' number.

That's strange, she thought. *My folks hardly ever call. And it's been ages since I called them,* she continued thinking as she picked up the phone. *They're so independent, almost self-sufficient to a fault.*

However, the voice on the other end was her mother saying, "Your dad just had a stroke and is in intensive care at Harbor General Hospital."

WORRYING ABOUT YOUR LIFESTYLE

Not only had Betty lived a charmed life at home with everything going so well, but she had also enjoyed a charmed relationship with her parents. They were the best parents a daughter could have! They had always been very supportive of everything Betty had done. They loved and admired her husband, Fred. (Yes, Betty knew that this was not always the case in families.) They doted over the grandkids and spoiled them rotten, in a good way, of course! They had never visited too often, and when they did, they didn't stay too long. They had never interfered in any way in Betty's life. They were the perfect parents!

But now, they weren't so perfect because they finally needed help from their only daughter. Betty's immediate thought was, *This couldn't have happened at a worse time!* Later she would confess this attitude to the Lord, but for now, she began a bout of worry that would last for some time. What should she do? Her thoughts went something like this: *I was the first woman to be promoted to this level. I can't let the company down, and I sure can't let the other women in the company down either.*

Then there's my family. Thank the Lord, things are great with Fred. He's been so understanding and supportive about everything. But the added pressure of my parents? Well, that'll be a new test I hope we pass! Then there are the children, who are already leaning on me to spend more time with the new grandbabies.

Her stomach was churning and her head was definitely spinning as Betty dashed out of the house. Worry moved in and continued throughout her hour-long commute to the office.

APPRECIATING YOUR PARENTS

Let's face it. We are basically selfish people.

At least that's what the Bible says in Romans 3:23 — "All have sinned." It's our nature. Many of us had wonderful parents, and while we were growing up, we happily took everything they provided. And we rarely took the time to notice the sacrifices they were making to ensure that we were well taken care of. Of course Betty appreciated her parents. And sure, she was worried. But truthfully, her first thoughts were focused on herself, and not so much on her parents! Basically she was worried that the new needs of her parents might conflict with her own blossoming success and plans for her already too-busy life.

> *What does "honoring our parents" mean? We are to respect and value them, consider it our God-given duty to be available to them, and help them as much as possible.*

I was a lot like Betty in the years after my marriage and the starting of a family. My parents were schoolteachers in Oklahoma until the day they retired. Yet somehow they managed to raise and put four children through college. Never mind that they both taught night classes on top of their day jobs and summer school on their vacation time. Never mind they took on other extra jobs to somehow raise and educate us. And never mind they each constantly chipped away at the course work needed to earn extra degrees and the certification required for additional raises in salary that would help them fulfill their goals for the four of us. It was only as I began to understand what the Bible says about my responsibility as a daughter that I began to truly appreciate their sacrifice.

Well, Betty hadn't reached this deeper level of appreciation yet. She was still stuck at the "take them for granted" level. She still operated under the principle that no news is good news. Oh, she did appreciate her parents, but not to the extent the Bible talks about.

HONOR YOUR PARENTS

Everyone loves a promise, especially if it enhances the quality of life. God has given us a promise in Ephesians 6:2–3, a promise originally delivered to God's people as one of the Ten Commandments. But in order to receive the blessings attached to that promise, we must follow the law that comes with it. First the law — "Honor your father and mother." Then the promise — "that it may be well with you and you may live long on the earth." In other words, God asks us to act on His command to honor our parents, and He assures us of a spiritually and physically blessed life when we do so.

This is where the saying "What goes around comes around" applies. We honor our parents, which provides a model and example for our children, and in turn, they care for us in our later lives. This is God's perfect plan for each family's well-being. And exactly what does "honoring our parents" mean? It means that we as children of any age are to respect, value, and see it as our God-given duty to be there for our parents as much as we're able as they have been there for us.

Fortunately, this is where most Christian women are. They do care and are deeply concerned about their parents' welfare. And they do also tend to worry about their parents. And to multiply their burdens, if they're married, they generally also take on the task of worrying for the welfare of their husbands' parents too.

PUTTING LOVE INTO ACTION

A beautiful instance of the loving devotion of a "child's" care for parents is the story of the daughter-in-law/mother-in-law relationship between Ruth and Naomi. We considered Ruth earlier as a giving and sacrificing widow, but she is also an outstanding model for following through on God's law to honor parents — and parents-in-law. I hope you'll treat yourself to a read through the little book of Ruth in the Old Testament. It will only take you about ten minutes.

Ruth wasn't even a blood relative to Naomi. No, she was a foreigner. But after the death of her husband, Naomi's son, Ruth faithfully lived out her love and devotion to, of all people, her mother-in-law! She honored, respected, valued, and took care of Naomi with actions like these.

Ruth left all to help her mother-in-law. When Naomi was alone after the death of her husband and two sons, Ruth pledged her loyalty to Naomi. "Entreat me not to leave you, or to turn back from following after you; for wherever you go, I will go . . . Where you die, I will die" (Ruth 1:16–17). No amount of restraint from Naomi could dissuade Ruth from following through on her resolve to be there for her mother-in-law.

What are you willing to sacrifice or give up for either or both sets of parents? Visiting your parents and in-laws takes time. Do you need to appropriate some time for a visit, a phone call, or a long email? Keeping in touch also requires money — money for gas, money for airline tickets, money for phone calls and Internet for email. Is money set aside in your budget for travel, chatting, and staying in touch so you can keep up with the day-in, day-out details of your parents' lives?

Ruth showed authentic devotion. Naomi encouraged her two daughters-in-law to go back to their homes and people. She completely released both women from any and all obligation to her. The other daughter-in-law chose to stay in her homeland. But Ruth refused to leave Naomi's side. Ruth even uttered an oath to seal her loyalty stating, "The LORD do so to me, and more also, if anything but death parts you and me" (verse 17).

What actions can you take to show your devotion to your parents and parents-in-law? Regular visits communicate loudly of your love and devotion and concern. Also assuring your parents of your interest in their welfare and your willingness to help with any of their needs speaks volumes. Then, when the time comes, be sure to follow through. Act on your words and intentions.

Ruth served her mother-in-law. Ruth's service extended to performing backbreaking work to provide for Naomi. "Please let me go to the field, and glean heads of grain" (Ruth 2:2).

How can you serve the parents in your two families? Some of my service to both my and Jim's parents included doing housework for them, washing and folding loads of clothes any time I was there, running errands, and picking up groceries. For Jim's mom, it extended to taking her to the oncologist, picking up prescriptions, and visiting the hospital. And that service included being at Lois' bedside as she passed into glory.

For my mom and dad, well, about seven years of my life were spent regularly weaving myself into their lives, traveling in a far-off state for visits to each of their nursing homes. True love and honor involves time and money for sure, but it also involves service as you take care of your parents' needs.

Ruth accepted advice. In Ruth we're allowed to see a truly humble and teachable daughter-in-law. Ruth was counseled by Naomi in the customs of the day in her new land. And she not only listened, but she did what was advised. She followed Naomi's counsel, and God honored Ruth's humility by securing a new and godly husband for her (Ruth 3).

How teachable are you? Can you listen and learn from parents and in-laws? Remember, "The way of a fool is right in his own eyes, but he who heeds counsel is wise," even if it's from your mother-in-law (Proverbs 12:15)!

Ruth accepted help. So often, especially in the early years of marriage, we want to prove our capability as a wife and later as a mom. To ask for or accept help is in our minds a show of weakness and incompetency. Not so with Ruth. When her first baby came along, the Bible paints this tender picture of her mother-in-law's willingness and desire to help: "Naomi took the child and laid him on her bosom, and became a nurse to him" (Ruth 4:16).

In what areas are you willing to let your parents help out? Maybe they're offering much-needed funds. Or they want to come help you with a project on your house. Or they would like to spend more time with you and the kids. Or they would love to babysit, or let you drop off the children while you go out.

On the flip side, if you are the parent, in what areas can you volunteer to help out in your children's lives? It was my utter delight (and still is) to be "Babysitter #1" for my daughters' little ones. I told them point-blank, "*Please* call me first. If it's at all humanly possible, I'll be there. I want to babysit! I want to give you a break for some time alone with your husband, some freedom to run errands, shop by yourself, or get a haircut." Another thing Jim and I were committed to was helping any time our girls moved . . . or had a baby . . . or had medical problems.

Doing Your Part

You may be deeply involved in your parents' lives. You know what's happening or not happening with them. You want to show honor and respect, to check up on them and check out your concerns for their well-being. This is the way it should be. But as we've acknowledged, if worry is all that results from your concerns, it will be of no benefit to you or your parents. It will not positively affect any of you.

The best way to deal with your concerns is by taking action. God may not be asking you to take the steps Ruth took. And your schedule and responsibilities may not allow you to take the steps I was able to take or others have taken. But God is asking you to care about, care for, love, and be involved in your parents' lives. Maybe today He's only asking you to be available if and when their needs arise. As with Betty, very little may be required of you for years. But unlike Betty, that shouldn't keep you from staying in close touch, being involved in their lives, and welcoming and encouraging their involvement in yours.

When it comes to parents, absence does not make the heart grow fonder. During the years and decades — the waiting years — that your parents are in good health, focus on feeding the fires of love for them. Here are a few things you can do now and plan to do. Then when the time comes and you are needed — and it will come! — your heart will be ready to spring into action on new and different fronts. You're probably a master planner. You have to be in order to keep everything and everyone in your every day running without a hitch. So put your mind to work on planning where your parents are concerned.

✓ *Plan to follow God's plan.* It's God's plan that you "honor your father and mother," which involves developing a mindset of obedience to His command to do so. Then you'll be ready when their call for help comes. You won't be like Betty, who had basically put her parents in the back closet of her life and was going about her own personal business.

Honoring my father is an action I took when my dad was dying in Oklahoma. I was willing to obey God's command when my "call for help" came. Because I didn't have a normal job like my three brothers did, my husband and I agreed I would fly from Los Angeles to Oklahoma every Monday and stay with my dad until Friday when one of my brothers could come to be with him through the weekend. Actually, Jim felt more strongly about this plan than I did. He felt it was one sure way to live out God's fifth commandment (Exodus 20:12). Our children were grown and married, so I had a settled peace about my commitment and all that it involved.

You can probably imagine what precious days those were that I spent with my dad. I will cherish those memories for the rest of my life. And I suffer no guilt and have no regrets for that season in my life. And this was not a short-term commitment. His cancer lingered for almost a year, so long that I was on a first-name basis with the Monday and Friday flight attendants on my airline. It was a financial sacrifice. But Jim and I determined that this was the way we could best honor my dad, and especially during his time of greatest need.

✓ *Plan to visit your parents.* It's one thing to talk about paying a visit to your parents and quite another to actually do it. If your parents are close by, try to schedule regular times to visit. If they live some distance away, it will probably take some advance planning to make this happen. I'm sure you've heard of people who say they can't visit their parents because they don't have the money. But amazingly many continue to eat fast food and dine out at restaurants, buy large-screen TVs, subscribe to cable, and purchase new cars.

If something is important to us, we must try to find a way to make it happen. So sit down with your family and map out a calendar and a budget to ensure regular visits with faraway parents. Just think what you are teaching your kids! Without a word, you're instructing your children about what it means to honor parents. One picture is truly worth a thousand words. And your children will remember your sacrifices when it comes to visiting you in the years to come.

✓ *Plan to call and write your parents often.* Put your mind to work on figuring out as many ways as you can for staying in touch with both sets of parents. And don't forget to involve your children in that planning. My married kids just talked Jim and me into getting new phones that have texting capabilities. What fun! Now my daughters and I stay in touch and carry on communication through text messages almost daily with very few words! Do whatever works best for you. Write, call, text, or Twitter! And don't be surprised if your kids don't always return communications right away. Remember when you were starting your family or were knee-deep in children of all ages? As you well know, it's a minute by minute, crisis by crisis challenge that can be all-consuming!

✓ *Plan to pray for your parents.* When you and your family gather around the dinner table, do you often offer up a vague, general prayer like, "God bless my parents and all the missionaries"? You know you should be praying for your parents, but because you have so little contact with them, you don't know anything specific to pray about. If you're in regular contact with them, your prayers will be based on what's really happening in their lives and their up-to-date needs. Always remember, you cannot neglect the person you are praying for. Your most recent efforts at staying in touch with Mom and Dad lead to your heartfelt prayers, which lead to your time, attention, and care.

> *Don't let the busyness and craziness of life keep you from living out God's plan that you love and honor your parents.*

✓ *Plan to send pictures.* Picture-taking is becoming easier and easier. Your cell phone probably already has a camera, or you can buy an inexpensive digital camera or even a disposable camera to carry in your purse. Just yesterday my daughter Katherine sent me a picture of her new hairstyle. I didn't have to wait until the next time I saw her. If your parents have Internet connection, send pictures on a regular basis, even daily. The point is, where there's a will, there's a way to keep your parents involved in your family's life. If you have film developed or subscribe to an on-line service, order duplicates of every picture and give them to both sets of parents.

✓ *Plan to seek your parents' advice.* Honor is respect, and what better way to show respect than to ask or receive advice from your parents or in-laws. Just look at how Moses honored his father-in-law in Exodus 18:13–26. Moses was judging the people all by himself. Jethro saw what was happening and said, "Both you and these people who are with you will surely wear yourselves out. For this thing is too much for you" (verse 18). His advice was that Moses pick qualified leaders to take on some of the responsibility of judging the people. Great advice! Just think what might have happened if Moses had refused Jethro's help.

Whether you're seeking advice on child-raising or a recipe for cherry pie or ideas on which brand of car to purchase, run things by your parents. My dad sub-scribed to — and read — the *Changing Times* magazine all his life. No wonder my three brothers and Jim and I were always asking him for his knowledge or opinion on the things that concerned us — loan rates, interest rates, best brand of refrigerator. You name it, he knew it!

Do your part. I know you're busy. And most of the time 24 hours in a day doesn't seem like enough. But if you look at those hours from a different angle, you do actu-ally have 24 hours in every day! So what's a five-minute phone call or two-minute email to your mom out of the vastness of 1440 minutes? It's practically nothing! And if you called or emailed your mother-in-law too, it's still not much. And what's five minutes on the Internet to see how much airfare is to your parents' house? You and I *can* do our part. Honestly, if we'll just *think* about our parents, that thinking will lead to doing something. Don't let the busyness and craziness of *your* life keep you from living out *God's* plan that you love and honor your parents. You will be blessed when you do . . . and so will your mom and dad.

Breaking the Worry Habit . . . Forever!

If we were living as our ancestors did, we would probably be near our parents. Our folks might even be living with us. So there would be little or no effort needed to know all about their daily lives and needs and exactly how to honor and care for them. But our twenty-first-century technological, mobile, fractured-family lifestyles have pushed us into bad habits that we may not be aware of.

As we've been learning, a habit is something that people do on a regular basis. It can be a good habit or a bad habit. One way to break the bad habit of worrying about your parents is to cultivate the good habit of staying in close touch with them. It's so easy to worry in a vacuum. Because we don't know what's really happening in our parents' lives, we worry about their health, their finances, their living alone or being homebound, the possibility of marital strife, their medical care, the potential of their being taken advantage of, and many other things.

Well, obviously this parental worry list can and does go on and on as your folks pass through various ages and stages. Being close to your parents gives you the information you need for acting on their behalf. Begin to strengthen the good habit of being involved in your parents' lives by paying attention to these four practices:

- Stay in touch.

- Know all that you can know.

- Do all that you can do.

- Pray faithfully about what you cannot do.

Honor your father and your mother,
as the LORD your God has commanded you,
that your days may be long,
and that it may be well with you.
DEUTERONOMY 5:16

10
WHAT WILL OTHERS THINK?

Am I now seeking the favor of men,
or of God?
Or am I striving to please men?
If I were still trying to please men,
I would not be a bond-servant of Christ.
GALATIANS 1:10 NASB

Maybe it was because she was an only child, but ever since she could remember, Lisa had tried to "fit in" wherever she went. Even as a child, Lisa wanted to be liked, so she made sure she didn't have an opinion of her own, for fear of being rejected. This often meant she had to compromise a little of herself and the Christian beliefs that had been instilled in her since childhood.

And this was especially true on this occasion! Lisa wasn't very pretty, or at least she didn't think she was. So when Bert started noticing her and offering compliments, Lisa was surprised and flattered. Then when he asked her out on a date, she was overwhelmed! Bert was nice, polite, and always a perfect gentleman. Their relationship moved along and, in the course of time, Bert asked if Lisa would marry him.

Like every girl, Lisa had daydreamed often about this moment, and having rehearsed her response for years, she said *yes!* Then came the opposing voices. "How can you marry him? He's not a Christian!" "But I love him. He's a good man, and I'm sure in time he'll come around." The problem with Lisa's logic was that subtly, oh so subtly, she had compromised her testimony to fit in and gain the approval of other people until there wasn't a lot of difference between her views and actions and Bert's. To please her man, Lisa had slipped badly in her Christian life.

It's True Confession Time

Think about Lisa's story. What was the result of her desire for approval? She was willing to go against her better judgment, the advice of others, and everything she'd been taught and knew from the Bible about "evangelistic dating" and marrying an unbeliever. Her story may be an extreme example of worrying about the approval of others. But whether it's a fear of rejection or persecution, or making a mistake or doing a poor job, or just a desire for approval and acceptance, a person who makes a compromising decision reaps painful consequences.

I grew up under the umbrella of "What will others think?" Whenever I did something foolish, I was confronted with "What will others think?" Even if what I did was good (having a job while attending college versus not having one, taking summer school classes instead of going home for the summer, waiting to have children versus starting a family right away), it was always the same question. "What will others think?"

> *No one is immune from the temptation to compromise beliefs and principles for the approval of others.*

When I consider the things I tend to worry about today, amazingly they fall into the category of ministry. I've read that fear of public speaking is right up at the top of many people's fear and worry list. And yet that's what God asks of me. I'm a good cookie baker, and I can sew and clean and set up and clean up. At church I've never had any problem serving. But a red-letter day arrived when I was asked to make an announcement in front of our couples' Bible class about a women's event. Immediately my mind started up. "What if I look silly or unprofessional?" "What if I stutter or stumble over my words . . . or forget one important detail?" "What if I fail?" Well, I did the announcement, and I did okay because I wrote it out and practiced for weeks, but I couldn't shake the doubt of what others thought afterward.

Then I was asked to share a ten-minute devotional at a women's luncheon at my church. And it all started up again. "What will others think . . . if I go too long . . . if I run out of things to say . . . if I don't make sense . . . if I lose my place . . . if I forget what I was going to say . . . if they don't think what I chose to wear was appropriate?"

And now one of my key ministries is speaking at women's conferences. And I can tell you I start down the what-will-others-think trail every single day leading up to every single conference. And every single day I have to come back to God. To center on God. To look full into His wonderful face. To get my eyes off others and onto Him. To remember He is the one asking me to do this — that it's not them (the women) but it's Him I must please.

I don't know where your weak spot is when it comes to desiring the approval and acceptance of others. But I do know that no one is immune from the temptation to compromise beliefs and principles for the approval of others or to sit on the sidelines in fear of what others will think, of how you will be judged, of what stepping out in obedience or speaking up might do to your reputation.

WORRY AND THE APPROVAL OF OTHERS

Look now at some people in the Bible who sought the approval of others, for whatever reason, whether worry or fear or pride. As you read, note what they desired more than they desired to do what God wanted them to do, and also note the consequences.

Abraham lied to save his life. He was a great prince in the land of Palestine, blessed by God with a beautiful wife, a multitude of servants, and numerous flocks and herds.

From the time God called Abraham to leave his homeland and follow Him, God had faithfully guided and protected Abraham and his household and livestock. But in a moment of fear for his own safety and fear of the disapproval of the pharaoh of Egypt, he asked his wife to lie about their marriage status. He coached Sarai (Sarah), "Please say you are my sister, that it may be well with me" (Genesis 12:13). Abraham risked the reputation of his wife and disregarded God's vow of protection and blessing (verse 2) because of his desire for the approval of a pagan king and his fear of being killed.

Isaac followed in the fearful footsteps of his father, Abraham. He too lied about his relationship with his wife, Rebekah, saying, " 'She is my sister'; for he was afraid to say, 'She is my wife.' " Like his father, Isaac was willing to disregard the reputation of his wife and the promises of God. Why? Because of a desire for the approval of others and his own well-being (Genesis 26:7).

King Saul failed to wait for a priest to offer the sacrifice to God. Saul was the first king of Israel. Physically he had the makings of a great king. He was tall, dark, and handsome, but . . . he had approval issues. Early in his kingship, the prophet Samuel instructed Saul to wait at a certain place for seven days until Samuel arrived to offer burnt offerings to unite the people before battle against the Philistines (1 Samuel 10:8). On the seventh day, when it looked as though Samuel had failed to show up, Saul saw the people scattering and feared a collapse of his battle plan. So Saul decided to offer the sacrifice himself and keep the people united. Of course, Samuel arrived as soon as Saul finished offering the sacrifice! Because of his desire for approval and acceptance as a leader by his troops, Saul's kingship was taken away and would later be given to David (1 Samuel 13:8–14).

The Jewish leadership feared Jesus. They were afraid Jesus would rally the people with His many miracles, resulting in greater oppression by the Roman government. This would mean these Jewish leaders would lose their favored positions. Because of their fear and greed and their desire for the approval of the Romans, these leaders plotted ways to kill Jesus, God's Son (John 11:45–53).

Pilate feared the crowds and the Jewish leadership. He wanted to keep his position as the governor of Judea, so much so that he washed his hands and allowed the crowds to dictate Jesus' punishment (Matthew 27:24).

The disciple Peter lied about knowing Jesus. After Jesus was betrayed and arrested, Peter followed Him into the courtyard of the high priest. This was a brave act, but it would be soon nullified. While he sat warming his hands by a fire, a servant girl recognized Peter as a disciple of Jesus. You know how the story goes, don't you? Peter denied three times that he knew Jesus. He feared being exposed and the persecution that might follow. Peter's desire for acceptance caused him to do a horrible, cowardly thing (Luke 22:54–62).

King Herod sought to please the Jewish leaders. The grandson of Herod the Great, this ruler had the disciple and apostle James put to death. This act immediately pleased the Jewish leaders of the day. Desiring even more approval and popularity with these leaders, Herod seized Peter and put him in prison, fully intending to have Peter killed as well (Acts 12:1–4). Like so many others, Herod's desire for approval caused him to do terrible things.

The apostle Peter gave in to peer pressure.

Years after Christians had moved and scattered from Jerusalem to other places, Peter visited a Gentile church at Antioch. While there, the apostle freely shared meals and fellowship with the Gentile believers. But when so-called Jewish authorities arrived from the church in Jerusalem, Peter began to withdraw from the Gentiles. He separated himself from them and would have nothing to do with them. The apostle Paul, who was also there, confronted Peter, accusing him of succumbing to the hypocrisy of the Jewish leaders. Peter knew better, but peer pressure and fear of disapproval and rejection by the Jews from Jerusalem had gotten the best of him (Galatians 2:11–14).

IT'S A MATTER OF PRIORITIES

This is a sad list of "men-pleasers," isn't it? And just look at the consequences they reaped! You and I must realize that pleasing men — pleasing others — will never have a good outcome. But when we put God first and desire to please Him and Him alone . . . well, that's a different story!

God requires first place in our lives. Jesus said it this way: "Take heed that you do not do your charitable deeds before men, to be seen by them. Otherwise you have no reward from your Father in heaven" (Matthew

6:1). So you and I have a choice to make. We've already seen some of the concessions people were willing to make in order to gain the favor of men. Now let's move toward the positive and look at some people who were willing to resist the temptation of gaining the approval of men. They were willing to suffer the world's disdain, disapproval, and wrath rather than willfully place God in a secondary — or lower — position in their lives. Their perfect love for God overruled all their fear of the disapproval and judgment of men. In the words of John, "There is no fear in love; but perfect love casts out fear" (1 John 4:18).

The apostle Paul lived to serve and please God. In the verse used at the beginning of this chapter, you read this very black-and-white statement:

Am I now seeking the favor of men, or of God? Or am I striving to please men? If I were still trying to please men, I would not be a bond-servant of Christ (Galatians 1:10 NASB).

Paul, like Jesus, is saying that putting God first is an either/or choice. You *either* serve God *or* you serve man.

195

Paul makes this either/or statement as he's writing a letter to the church in Galatia, which he founded on his first missionary journey. He had heard that false teachers were spreading a "different gospel" throughout Galatia, and sadly, the people were buying into their heretical teaching. So Paul opens his letter with strong words of condemnation for those who would preach a false gospel message (verses 8–9). Then in verse 10 he gives a justification for his stern language. He says he wouldn't have uttered these grim words if he had been "striving to please men." He would have preached a watered-down gospel. But that would be an affront to God. Paul wasn't concerned about the approval of his readers. He was concerned about the approval of God.

Paul continued this focus on God throughout his years of ministry. After his third and final missionary journey, he headed toward Jerusalem to fulfill a vow he had made to God. Along the way he was warned by a group of believers, including a number of prophets, that if he proceeded to Jerusalem, he would be captured and put into prison. But Paul stayed true to his plan to complete his vow. He resisted the temptation to listen to the fears of others and determined to continue on to Jerusalem. To those who wished to sway Paul's resolve, he stated: "I am ready not only to be bound, but also to die at Jerusalem for the name of the Lord Jesus" (Acts 21:13).

Why did Paul have such a great impact on his generation? Perhaps it was his passionate desire and solid resolve to serve his Lord . . . period . . . no matter what . . . regardless of the suffering he would experience because of it (2 Corinthians 11:23–28).

Daniel said no to a king. There he was, a teenaged captive in a foreign land. Daniel's parents were probably dead, killed by his captors. Once he was established in his new country, Daniel was asked to do a very small thing, even a nice thing — eat a special, privileged diet offered to all the trainees who might ultimately become government officials. No biggie, right? Well, to Daniel it was a watershed moment. Would he give in? Would he gain the acceptance of this new people, and win the approval of his new king, and not make waves? Would he seek to draw positive attention to himself rather than standing out as a dissenter? Would he just go with the flow and possibly land a cushy job with the government? Here's the decision Daniel made:

Daniel purposed in his heart that he would not defile himself with the portion of the king's delicacies, nor with the wine which he drank; therefore he requested of the chief of the eunuchs that he might not defile himself (Daniel 1:8).

Daniel was willing to suffer the consequences of his decision, which might even include death. But he made his decision. He "purposed in his heart" to gain the approval of God rather than men. In the end God, our wonderful, powerful God, protected him and gave him wisdom and visions of the future, which he recorded in chapters 7 through 12 of the book of Daniel. God also gave him great honor and influence with three different kings during his long life.

The three friends of Daniel made a tough decision too. They were also teens who were taken captive by the Babylonians. They too were asked to make a choice — bow down to a statue of the king or face death by fire (Daniel 3:4–18). Listen to their resolve, spoken while they stood before the most powerful man on the face of the earth as he commanded them to bow down or suffer death:

If that is the case, our God whom we serve is able to deliver us from the burning fiery furnace, and He will deliver us from your hand, O king. But if not, let it be known to you, O king, that we do not serve your gods, nor will we worship the gold image which you have set up (Daniel 3:17–18).

These three God-centered young men were willing to suffer the consequence of an ugly death for their commitment to God. You see, to them it didn't matter what might be done to them. Pleasing a heathen king was low on their list — in fact, not on it at all. No, all that mattered to these true followers of God was pleasing Him.

Peter and John faced the Jews without fear. Earlier in their relationship with Jesus, when Jesus was arrested, these two men abandoned their Lord out of fear of man and the consequences of following Christ (Matthew 26:56). Yet in time they boldly stood before the religious leaders without fear of persecution or rejection or death. There they uttered this declaration: "Whether it is right in the sight of God to listen to you more than to God, you judge. For we cannot but speak the things which we have seen and heard" (Acts 4:19–20).

Stephen died with dignity, becoming the first martyr for Christ. Due to his fearless love and devoted service to God, Stephen ended up standing before the council of scribes and elders. There he was falsely accused of speaking "blasphemous words against this holy place and the law" (Acts 6:13). Not only did Stephen die unjustly, but he also prayed at his death for the forgiveness of his executioners, "Lord, do not charge them with this sin" (Acts 7:60).

Doing Your Part

A habit is a learned behavior. When you do something once, and then again . . . and again . . . and again, it becomes routine, an ingrained part of your life. As we've been learning, worry is a bad habit that we've learned over a period of time. So if we can learn a bad habit, guess what? We can unlearn it and replace it with a good one. Our goal is to replace worrying about the approval of others with a genuine desire to gain the approval of God.

How do you avoid the mental anguish and worry that comes with the temptation to give in to peer pressure, fear of rejection, or fear of persecution? It's not easy, is it? We've all been there, and maybe we're still there. But it doesn't have to continue. No, there is hope and help for us. If others have broken and unlearned this worry and fear habit of needing approval, you and I can too! Here are some things you can do, as always, with God's help.

✓ *Keep your focus on God.* No runner ever wins a race while distracted by the crowds in the stands. He keeps his eyes riveted on the track and the finish line in front of him. The writer of Hebrews encourages us to "run with endurance the race that is set before us, looking unto Jesus, the author and finisher of our faith" (Hebrews 12:1–2). If your focus is on pleasing Christ, you will always say and do the right thing, the God-honoring thing. Compromise will never be an issue! Always remember, compromise serves men, while commitment serves God.

✓ *See yourself as dead to self.* As a believer you are identified with Christ both in His death and in His resurrection. The apostle Paul explains and exhorts: "Likewise you also, reckon yourselves to be dead indeed to sin, but alive to

God in Christ Jesus our Lord. Therefore do not let sin reign in your mortal body, that you should obey it in its lusts" (Romans 6:11–12). If you see yourself as dead to yourself, along with all your pride, fears, feelings of loneliness, and yearning of acceptance, you

> *There is no limit to what God can do in and through you, including helping you withstand the temptation to compromise.*

won't be tempted to conform to the world's standards. In other words, there is no *you*. There is only *Christ*. As the Bible says, "I have been crucified with Christ; it is no longer I who live, but Christ lives in me; and the life which I now live in the flesh I live by faith in the Son of God, who loved me and gave Himself for me" (Galatians 2:20).

✓ *Accept your eternal citizenship.* The temptation for worldly acceptance comes when you lose sight of your identity. As a believer in Christ you are a kingdom citizen (Philippians 3:20). You are a sojourner and a pilgrim (1

Peter 2:11), merely passing through this life on your way to eternity. So don't get too settled in a world and a life that is passing away. This will keep you from worrying and being overly concerned about what people think of you and your Christian standards and beliefs.

✓ *Pray for personal boldness.* The apostles in the early church weren't any different than you and me. They had their fears of persecution. But they took their worry and concerns to God in prayer (Acts 4:23–30). What was the result of their prayers? "And when they had prayed, the place where they were assembled together was shaken; and they were all filled with the Holy Spirit, and they spoke the word of God with boldness" (Acts 4:31). They went from being a fearful group to being a bold force for God. They were no longer worrying about themselves. Their priority was God. The result? They literally turned the world upside down for Jesus!

✓ *Realize you are empowered by Christ.* Putting God first is not easy. In fact, it's never been easy for any Christian in any age. But God has given us a secret weapon, the Holy Spirit. God is able to answer your prayers and help you through the power of the working of the Spirit in your life. The extent of this power is determined by your yieldedness to the Holy Spirit. So in a sense you determine what God is able to do through you. In His ability, there is no limit to what He can do in and through you, including empowering you to withstand the temptation to compromise. That's the message to us in Ephesians 3:20: "Now to Him who is able to do exceedingly abundantly above all that we ask or think, according to the power that works in us."

God is fully able to enable you to live a victorious Christian life. And He is willing and available to do so. That's His part. Now it's up to you to do your part, to focus fully on Him — not others — and live for Him.

Breaking the Worry Habit . . . Forever!

God created you as a social being. He said, "It is not good that man should be alone" (Genesis 2:18). Maybe this is why so many people are habitually worrying about their relationships. They don't want to be alone. And they don't want to be left out. They want friends, and they want to belong. Where does this book find you today? Is seeking the approval of other people at the top of your current "worry list"? Are you constantly worrying, "What will others think . . . of me, of how I look, of what I'm wearing, of where I live, of what I'm doing or not doing"?

If you are worrying about belonging and the approval of others, consider what it's costing you. Are your desires for approval turning you away from God and from following Him? If so, then you have every right to be worried. Not about your earthly relationships, but about your relationship with your heavenly Father. I hope this chapter and these truths have reminded you that, if you have a relationship with God through His Son, the Lord Jesus, you have the best of all relationships. If Jesus is your Savior, He is also your Friend. Seek His favor above all others. Then you will always have at least one friend, the best of all friends, the ultimate friend. Even if everyone else forsakes you, God is there. Why worry about the approval of others when you have Jesus as your "friend who sticks closer than a brother" (Proverbs 18:24)?

The LORD is my helper;
I will not fear.
What can man do to me?
HEBREWS 13:6

11
What Is the Right Thing to Do?

If any of you lacks wisdom,
let him ask of God,
who gives to all liberally and
without reproach,
and it will be given to him.

JAMES 1:5

Anita had finally made a decision. She ordered her first-ever computer! The process had been agonizing because she wanted to do the right thing. And she wanted to be a good steward of God's money. So she had labored long and hard in prayer. After painstaking research and asking anyone and everyone she knew who might advise her — even her gardener and the lady who did her nails — she had done it! She screwed up her courage, said a short "Help me, Lord" prayer, and called the order line of a well-known mail-order computer company. They walked her through the process. She told them what she needed for her small business and personal needs, and they literally built her computer just for her from the ground up! Exhausted from the ordeal, Anita decided to go to bed.

Then it happened. At two o-clock Anita woke up and sat straight up in bed with a severe anxiety attack. Had she done the right thing? The computer had cost a lot of money. What if she had bought the wrong one? It was built to her specifications, so unless it malfunctioned, she just might end up stuck with a useless *and* very expensive piece of electronics! Finally at five o'clock she gave up on sleep and rolled out of bed, still worrying if she had made the right decision. Did she do the right thing?

WORRY — IT'S A GOOD THING!

I'm sure you've heard the expression, "There's an exception to every rule." Well, I'm about to give you one exception to Jesus' command: "Do not worry."

For the past ten chapters, I've been hammering away at the concept of breaking the worry habit forever. But this is one of the times when worry is a good thing! You should always be concerned when it comes to decision making and making right choices. Your utmost concern should be to always try to make the decisions that will please God, the decisions that are His will.

I know I don't have to tell you the importance of making right decisions. Perhaps you realize today that you weren't as concerned about your decisions in the past as you should have been and, as a result, you made some bad choices. But now you know you don't want to make any more. In the past, you may have made some poor financial decisions, and now you want to be a good steward when it comes to buying a computer, a car, a home, or whatever else you may be considering. Perhaps you've made some less than godly decisions in the years gone by, and now you want to make decisions that will cause you to grow spiritually, help instead of harm others, and honor God with your life, your time, your relationships, and your actions. You want to make right decisions in the physical, social, financial, and spiritual areas. Well, now it's time to be concerned and worried in a good way about *every* decision you make — not just the big ones, but also the smaller ones. Who knows if the little decision made today won't turn into a major life-change tomorrow?

DECISION-MAKING BLUNDERS FROM THE BIBLE

Can you imagine anyone waking up tomorrow morning and saying, "How many wrong decisions can I make today?" Or "How many choices can I make that will do harm to me or one of my loved ones?" Or "How many decisions can I make today that will dishonor God and be a personal affront to His holiness?"

And yet, in many cases that's exactly what happens when we don't take decision making seriously, when we make decisions without thinking or asking advice of others, and especially when we don't take our choices to God. The Bible shows us many examples of people who made poor decisions. Do you think God is trying to tell us something? Let's learn what He does have to say through these men and women who failed to make good and wise decisions and reaped terrible consequences.

Eve. The "first lady" of Scripture had to

decide whether she would believe God and do what He said or listen to the lies of the serpent, the devil. We know the choice she made . . . and its consequences, because we and all mankind now live with the outcome of her wrong choice — the first one ever made in history. Eve questioned and doubted God's instructions not to eat the fruit from one specific tree in the entire garden of Eden. God had said, "Of every tree of the garden you may freely eat; but of the tree of the knowledge of good and evil you shall not eat" (Genesis 2:16–17). However, Eve chose to disobey God, ate the forbidden fruit, shared it with her husband Adam, and together they plunged the world into sin (Genesis 3).

Abraham. This "father of the Jewish nation" chose to ask his wife, Sarah, to lie about their marital status. Why would he do that? He was afraid. He asked Sarah, "Please say you are my sister" (Genesis 12:13). But in spite of a bad decision, God intervened and fulfilled His promise to make Abraham a great nation through Sarah.

Lot. Abraham's nephew Lot was asked to choose between the grassy land of the Jordan valley and the hill country to pasture his cattle. The right, common-sense choice was obvious — pick the well-watered valley, right? Wrong! The valley and its wicked cities of Sodom and Gomorrah ultimately corrupted Lot's family. In the end he lost all his possessions, his wife, and the morality and respect of his two daughters. These consequences add up to a sky-high price paid for a wrong decision (Genesis 13:10–13; 19).

Moses. God's chosen leader, Moses made several blunders in decision making. As a privileged young man, Moses chose to take matters into his own hands in order to protect a Hebrew slave.

> *Decisions based on emotions usually lead to more difficult situations or make matters worse.*

He killed the Egyptian who was beating the slave. Then, "when Pharaoh heard of this matter, he sought to kill Moses." Immediately Moses fled into the wilderness where he stayed for 40 years (Exodus 2:11–15). Later while leading all God's people during a 40-year trek through desert lands, Moses was commanded by God to "speak to the rock before their eyes, and it will yield its water; thus you shall bring water for them out of the rock, and give drink to the congregation and their animals" (Numbers 20:8). However, out of anger over the rebellious and complaining attitude of the people, Moses chose to strike the rock, not just once, but twice (verses 10–11). That decision to go against God's explicit instructions cost Moses the privilege of taking the people into the promised land (verse 12). He was allowed to look at it from afar but not to set foot in it. Moses' two wrong choices send a message to us across time — don't make decisions based on emotions! Make decisions based on doing God's will.

Orpah. This daughter-in-law to Naomi was encouraged by Naomi to return to her family after the death of Orpah's husband (also Naomi's son). Naomi, now a widow, decided to return to her native land Israel and to her own people. Orpah made the easy and humanly logical choice to do what Naomi offered . . . and was never heard of or mentioned in the Bible again. By contrast Ruth, Naomi's other daughter-in-law, made a harder and spiritual choice to leave her family, culture, and religion and cling to Naomi. She returned with Naomi, saying, "Your people shall be my people, and your God, my God" (Ruth 1:16). Ruth later married a man whose genealogy placed her offspring in the line of King David and ultimately the line of the Messiah.

David. This second king of Israel chose to commit adultery and murder. The results of these heinous decisions? The death of the child conceived during his adulterous relationship, the death of another of David's sons, incest within his family, and civil war in his kingdom. All this because of a few wrong decisions (2 Samuel 12–20)!

I'm sure you're getting the picture. A single wrong decision can lead to sin and change the course of our lives forever. Decisions based on fear, greed, emotion, and lust negatively affect the lives of others too. Even a relatively small decision (like David's choosing to continue to look at the woman who was bathing, the woman with whom he later committed adultery) can scar and mar many other people.

MOTIVES BEHIND DECISION MAKING

Have you ever analyzed what prompts you to make a particular decision? Very few, if any, decisions, are made in a vacuum. There's always something that provokes you or me to do what we do. Run through this short list of motives and emotions that contribute to many of the choices people make. Some are noble . . . and others are not so noble.

> *Fear* caused one of three servants who were given money to manage, save, and invest for their master to hide the money in the ground instead of invest it (Matthew 25:25).

> *Greed* moved Judas to betray Jesus and arrange for His capture . . . all for 30 pieces of silver (Matthew 26:15).

> *Love* led the already married Jacob to also marry his wife's sister, Rachel, causing strife and division in his family for generations (Genesis 29:20).

> *Loyalty* strengthened Jonathan to choose to defend his friend David to his father, the king, and to remain loyal to David after David fled for his life (1 Samuel 20:42).

> *Hatred* motivated Cain to murder his brother Abel after God rejected his offering and accepted Abel's sacrifice (Genesis 4:6–8).

> *Popularity* pleased Pilate so much that

he gave up on seeking to free Jesus and gave Him over to the murderous crowd (John 19:12).

- *Persecution* influenced Peter to choose to deny Jesus three times out of fear (Matthew 26:69–74).

- *Approval* induced Herod the king to kill the apostle James, and when he saw that it pleased the Jews, he tried to kill Peter too (Acts 12:1–4).

- *Obedience* fueled Daniel's choice to reject the king's food rather than break God's laws (Daniel 1:8).

- *Disobedience* spurred Jonah to choose to go in the opposite direction of Nineveh after God commanded him to go to Nineveh to preach against the people's sin (Jonah 1:1–3).

Doing Your Part

Now it's your turn. It's time to change or fine-tune how you're going to choose to make your decisions from now on. As I've already said, being concerned about making the right and best decisions is a good thing. If you can learn to take a few preliminary steps before rushing into something, or before choosing rashly or emotionally or without consideration, then you can be less worried and more confident that you're making right choices. Based on the right and wrong decisions made by this lineup of people and what motivated their choices, here are some steps you can take and some things you can do:

✓ *Review each decision.* Clarify exactly what is being asked of you. One way to sort things out is to pray. Review your situation before God. Ask for His guidance and discernment. Another way is to ask others, those who would know the answers or point you toward them. Eve should have asked Adam to review exactly what God had said to him about not touching and eating the fruit! If she had, Adam could have told her God's explicit command. Adam could have powerfully discredited what the devil was saying. Who makes up your corps of counselors? Who has God placed in your life that you can run things by before you make your decisions? Your pastor, your husband, an older woman, a mentor, your dad? Proverbs, the book of wisdom, teaches us that . . .

Where there is no counsel, the people fall; but in the multitude of counselors there is safety (11:14).

Without counsel, plans go awry, but in the multitude of counselors they are established (15:22).

By wise counsel you will wage your own war, and in a multitude of counselors there is safety (24:6).

✓ *Refine your options.* Beware of making a decision with only one option. It's probably the wrong one! Moses saw only one option — kill the Egyptian. For decades Jim served on our church's leadership board, where he had many opportunities to participate in making decisions that affected our entire church body. He was impressed by one chairman who never entertained a vote on something that had only one option. Meeting after meeting he sent the board members home to come up with other options to consider. Who's on

> *I've learned that if my heart is quiet and focused on doing God's will (not mine) and being led by Him (not my emotions, desires, or ambitions), then most of my decisions reflect His will and purpose.*

your "board"? Always take the option of looking for options — godly options, good, better, and best options. Read on.

✓ *Remember God's Word.* Get in the habit of asking yourself, "What does the Bible say about different options and their consequences?" The Bible is your standard. If any option doesn't agree with Scripture, it's a bad option. Therefore, it's out. When Jesus was tempted by Satan to not trust the Father, He chose to do battle with the weapon of the sword of the Spirit — the word of God (Ephesians 6:17). He stood firm, citing three different passages out of God's Word (Luke 4:4–12). If you're constantly in touch with God's Word — reading it, studying it, and memorizing it — then you're more likely to remember it when you need it.

It will be a sharply honed tool the Holy Spirit can use to guide you. How's your intake of God's Word? "The testimony of the LORD is sure, making wise the simple" (Psalm 19:7).

✓ *Restrain your emotions.* When people are upset, fearful, intimidated, mad, or sad, wrong decisions are sure to be made. (Remember the examples of Cain, Moses, Pilate, and Peter?) If you're suffering from any of the above, put your decision making on pause. Get your emotions under control by praying and seeking advice. Then approach your choices with a clear head and a heart that's calm and unclouded by feelings.

One goal I have in decision making is to be neutral. That doesn't mean I don't care about pleasing God or I don't care about the people involved. No, I care about them fiercely. But I've learned that if my heart is still, wishing only to do God's will (and not mine) and be led by Him (and not my emotions, desires, and ambitions), then there's nothing I want more than to make God's choice. I aim for a take-it-or-leave-it attitude.

Then I'm less likely to be swayed by greed, ambition, retaliation, pride, and temptation. If I can honestly consider something (like something to own, to do, to accept, to bear, to desire, to respond to) and say of that something, "I can take it or leave it. I can live with it or without it," I'm better able to choose God's direction.

✓ *Re-examine your motives.* Motives are deceptive. Amazingly we can justify almost anything! Our hearts are "wicked" and can easily deceive us into making wrong decisions (Jeremiah 17:9). When you get down to the business of making a decision, ask yourself, "Am I doing this or wanting this because it's the right thing to do or want, or because it's what I want?" God specifically told Jonah to go to Nineveh and preach for Him. But Jonah wanted what Jonah wanted! He didn't want to preach in Nineveh because the people there were his country's enemies and they just might respond to God's message. Once Jonah submitted to what God wanted, the people of Nineveh listened to Jonah's words, repented, and humbly turned to God.

Do you do what you do because it's what God wants you to do, or do you strike out on your own — out of God's will — and do your own thing? It helps me to recall these words which I carry with me always in my heart. Spoken by the apostle Paul, they remind me of who I am and who I belong to and what my "mission" on earth is — "the God to whom I belong and whom I serve" (Acts 27:23).

✓ *Recount your resources.* God has already given you "all things that pertain to life and godliness" (2 Peter 1:3). You have all the resources you will ever need to make right decisions and live out God's will. You have the wise counsel of God's people to help in your decision-making process. You have God's Spirit, who is your teacher and guide, and you have God's promises of . . .

- courage when you're fearful (Joshua 1:9)
- strength when you're weak (Philippians 4:13)
- His presence when you feel alone (Matthew 28:20)
- success when you fear failure

(Joshua 1:8)
- victory when you fear defeat (1 Corinthians 15:57)

Whatever you might fear, need, or think of . . . or worry about, God has already provided above and beyond what you can ask or think. Your God "shall supply all your need according to His riches in glory by Christ Jesus" (Philippians 4:19).

✓ *Resist impatience.* So often we're in a hurry to do something, purchase something, or go somewhere. This is where prayer comes to your rescue. How? Prayer makes you wait. Prayer slows you down. Prayer puts on the brakes. Then you can pray about the decision. As you do, prayer resurfaces your dependence on God and reminds you of His power and provision. Prayer also reveals your motives. Prayer searches your heart. Prayer pinpoints wrong motives. As I've learned through the years to pray about my decisions, some guiding principles have now become personal slogans I use to help me make good, better, and best choices. They point me in the right direction, whether it's beginning the process of decision making or dealing with doubts or an unsettled heart.

- No decision made without prayer (Philippians 4:6–7).
- When in doubt, don't (Romans 14:23).
- Always do what you know is right (James 4:17).
- Don't let fear influence you (1 John 4:18).

As you take the time and care to pray, there's never a need to worry about anything, including a decision you must make. Just pray! Prayer is your path to peace of mind.

✓ *Respond and make the decision.* If the above six steps have been followed, you should be confident that the decision you're making is a good one. Why? Because you're choosing to follow God's leading. You're not making decisions on your own. You're choosing instead to make God the essential element in your decision-making process. Even though, like our friend Betty, there may be doubts and bouts of worry, you can fall back on your decision and a thorough decision-making process with confidence.

Breaking the Worry Habit . . . Forever!

I know this section is reserved for addressing worry as a bad habit and ways and means of breaking that habit. But when it comes to being in God's will, doing what's right, and making godly decisions, worry is a good thing. I like to call it "good worry."

Everyone makes and must make decisions. And there are obviously a variety of levels of decisions to be made. Anita's decision was about a computer, a piece of machinery. But maybe you're having to decide whether to homeschool your children or not, whether it's time to admit an aging parent into a nursing home or not, whether to change churches or not, whether to submit to chemotherapy or not. Each and every decision you make, regardless of its level of intensity, is vitally important as you seek to do God's will. And that's exactly what decision making is — seeking to do God's will so you live in God's will. So pray! Involve God in your choices. He *will* guide you! As this chapter's opening truth stated, "If any of you lacks wisdom, let him ask of God . . . and it will be given to him" (James 1:5).

Follow the pattern set forth in Scripture. See each decision as important. Don't let even the small decisions — the minuscule or seemingly unimportant ones — slip by without consulting God. When you seek the Lord's will with all your heart and follow His leading, you're able to set aside worry and anxiety. You can bask in the peace of God, which surpasses all comprehension. You can enjoy peace in your heart and mind as you live God's will.

Be anxious for nothing, but in everything by prayer and supplication, with thanksgiving, let your requests be made known to God; and the peace of God, which surpasses all understanding, will guard your hearts and minds through Christ Jesus.

PHILIPPIANS 4:6–7

12

You Can Run, but You Can't Hide

*I acknowledged my sin to You,
and my iniquity I have not hidden.
I said, "I will confess my transgressions
to the LORD."*

PSALM 32:5

From the moment she watched the salesclerk swipe her credit card, Carol knew making her purchase was the wrong thing to do. But "oh, these pants are so fabulous . . . and just my size!" As a last resort in justifying herself, Carol proudly concluded, "and I saved 50 percent off the retail price!" So what if she and her husband Joe had committed as a couple to a spending freeze to get their finances under control? She just had to have those cool pants.

Back at home, she desperately tried to think of the best place to hide her treasured find. Her mind was also reeling with its latest assignment — trying to figure out what to do about breaking the news to Joe. Carol was well on her way to a full-out worryfest from the guilt she was experiencing. The whole ordeal was making her sick in both body and spirit.

Carol's transgression wasn't all that bad. After all, she hadn't killed anyone or stolen anything. It was just a little thing . . . or was it? If it was just a little thing, why was she so miserable? Why was she fretting so? Could it be that her conscience was talking to her? Was it because her God-instilled conscience was letting her know she'd done something wrong? Based on what her conscience was telling her, Carol's worries were justified!

Thank God for a Moral Compass!

As we step into this chapter, remember that in the previous chapter we considered what I labeled "good worry." Well, here's another area that falls into the "good worry" category. Guilt over sin is definitely a life issue you and I need to worry about in a good way. Whenever we offend God's holy character (which is sin), we should be deeply concerned. Whenever we're holding on to a sin or sinful practice and refusing to acknowledge or give it up, we should care profoundly.

If you really think about it, we should be thankful for a conscience. It's that inner voice that reminds us when we've done something wrong, when we've failed to live up to God's standards for His people. It's the prick of conviction that leads us to do the right thing and walk in all God's ways.

A more formal dictionary definition describing the conscience might read, "a person's moral sense of right and wrong, chiefly as it affects their own behavior." The Bible describes the role this moral compass plays in these ways:

- The conscience regulates the actions of all men based on the law of God written in their hearts (Romans 2:15).

- The conscience is purified at salvation (Hebrews 9:14).

- The conscience requires your effort to be kept pure (Acts 24:16).

- The conscience of another is to be respected in nonessential areas like dietary habits, etc. (1 Corinthians 8).

- The conscience is sometimes our best guide in areas where the Bible is silent (James 4:17).

- The conscience of a believer desires to act honorably in all things (Hebrews 13:18).

- The conscience that is pure reflects Christlikeness and deflects slander (1 Peter 3:16).

I hope you can see how important your conscience is in prompting you to better, more godly actions. But because of the sin nature of all mankind, your conscience cannot be your sole source of guidance. Sin causes us to deny reality and justify our actions according to man's standards. Therefore you must guard your conscience. It must be nurtured, cultivated, and protected so it confirms and validates God's Word, which is the ultimate lamp for lighting the path of your life (Psalm 119:105). And, I might add, for keeping you from a lot of worry and grief!

"You Feel Guilty Because You Are Guilty"

Have you ever heard this saying: "You feel guilty because you are guilty"? Well, guilt is the voice of your conscience. Guilt is your conscience talking to you, telling you that you *are* guilty. And guilt is not something new. No, it's been around a long, long time. It arrived hand in hand with the first sin ever committed, and it occurred in the perfection of the garden of Eden (Genesis 3). Consider the many lessons we learn from Adam and Eve about temptation, sin, guilt, and forgiveness.

Beware of temptation. You probably know Eve's story. She was tempted by the serpent (the devil) to eat the fruit from the one forbidden tree in the garden of Eden. The Bible tells us . . .

When the woman [Eve] saw that the tree was good for food, that it was pleasant to the eyes, and a tree desirable to make one wise, she took of its fruit and ate. She also gave to her husband with her, and he ate. Then the eyes of both of them were opened, and they knew that they were naked (verses 6–7).

Notice the progression of Eve's fall into

sin as she gave in to temptation. She saw the fruit. She snatched the fruit. She snacked on the fruit. She shared the fruit. Her sin was complete!

The slide into sin often starts with a second glance, a second thought, a question, or a hesitation. Then there's the rationalization that the option in front of you is something you not only want but something you think you need . . . and even deserve! When you reach this point, you're usually a goner, and the battle against temptation is lost.

Be aware of sin's consequences. Some of the first effects of committing an offense against God are guilt, shame, trying to hide what we did . . . and trying to hide from God. After sinning, Adam and Eve felt guilt and shame over their nakedness and tried to hide. Running from and avoiding God is an indicator of guilt about something. But, as the title of this chapter says, you can run, but you cannot hide. David wrote in one of his

> *Very few sins are isolated . . . Everyone knows of instances where others were devastated because of one person's sin.*

psalms, "Where can I flee from Your presence?" And the answer? Nowhere. As David acknowledged, "If I ascend into heaven, You are there; if I make my bed in hell, behold, You are there" (Psalm 139:7–8).

If you are running from God, it's best to give it up now. And don't even think about hiding. God loves you! Like the father of the prodigal son, He is waiting to welcome you, to celebrate your return, to fellowship with you (Luke 15:11–24). Run to Him now.

I can't leave this topic without mentioning another serious consequence of sin — it impacts other people. One of the alarming realities of sin is that its effects often spread like the first case of measles in a class of preschoolers! You see, no sin is isolated. Every sin is compounded as it hurts and involves others. After Eve sinned, she invited Adam to share in her rebellion, which then spread to all mankind (Romans 5:12). Everyone knows of some instance where other people were devastated because of one person's sin — an unfaithful husband or wife who brought sorrow and division to their family, a young adult child who committed a crime and brought heartache and shame to his family. Every sin is an act of total selfishness, and yet it always harms someone else.

Be quick to acknowledge sin. Guilt must be owned. Adam and Eve were guilty. That's that! But amazingly both of them tried to blame others for what they had done. Adam blamed Eve (and God too) — "The woman whom You gave to be with me, she gave me of the tree, and I ate" (Genesis 3:12). Eve then blamed the serpent — "The serpent deceived me, and I ate" (verse 13).

The worst step you or I can take when we slip up and sin is to try to eliminate our sin and guilt by blaming others or rationalizing the cause and seriousness of our failures. When we sin, we're guilty whether we own our actions or not. Only sin that is owned and acknowledged leads to repentance.

My husband has a saying we both try to live by: "Keep a short account with God." In other words, be constantly confessing sin . . . any sin . . . every sin (1 John 1:9). When we fail to acknowledge, admit, and deal with wrong words, actions, thoughts, and deeds, we are failing to walk with God. Our fellowship and communion with Him are broken. But as soon as we are repentant, the barrier between us and God is removed, and our joy and usefulness is restored. Once again we possess His strength and power for godly living.

Be free! You don't ever need to live a day or a minute or a second in bondage to sin. When you received Christ as your Savior, He set you free from the bondage of sin. Yet when we sin and fail to seek forgiveness, we are miserable. Our spiritual health and growth comes to a screeching halt. That's why guilt must be dealt with. King David is an example of one who failed to own and acknowledge his sin of adultery with Bathsheba (2 Samuel 11). For one entire year David struggled with his guilt and sin. Of this period of rebellion, he writes:

When I kept silent, my bones grew old through my groaning all the day long. For day and night Your hand was heavy upon me; my vitality was turned into the drought of summer (Psalm 32:3–4).

Can't you just hear David's agony? It was not until David owned, acknowledged, repented of, and confessed his sin that his guilt was removed and his sin forgiven. He was free!

I acknowledged my sin to You, and my iniquity I have not hidden. I said, "I will confess my transgressions to the LORD," and You forgave the iniquity of my sin (Psalm 32:5).

235

Be glad when guilty feelings spring up! And be concerned if you're not worried or sorry about your sinful actions. Your conscience and your feelings of guilt make you aware of your sin so you can, like David, acknowledge your sin to God, be freed by His forgiveness, and experience the joy of the Lord once again.

"JESUS PAID IT ALL"

I love these words from a powerful hymn from the past — "Jesus paid it all." These words and the entire hymn describe Christ's work on behalf of His followers.[1] From the very first transgression in the garden of Eden, God is seen as a merciful and saving God. He spared Adam and Eve from an eternally fallen state by removing them from the garden. He took away their shame by clothing them in the skins of animals. But this was only temporary. Guilt from sin had to be removed perma-

As your guilty conscience reminds you, go to Christ, acknowledge your wrongdoing, and agree with Him that what you've done is unacceptable. Christ is faithful to remove your sin.

nently. How was this accomplished? Enter God's Son, the Lord Jesus Christ! From the moment of Jesus' death, guilt and sin were taken care of.

Guilt is resolved through Christ. God Himself provided a permanent solution for sin and its crippling guilt. Jesus Christ, God's Son and the Lord, came to earth to be the perfect and complete sacrifice for sin. When people put their faith and trust in Christ and His death for their sins, they are made right with God (Romans 5:1). God, the righteous judge, declares them "not guilty" (Romans 8:1–2).

Guilt is removed in confession to Christ. Christ's death on the cross resolved the issue of sin and guilt. But there is also the problem of the removal of ongoing and daily guilt brought about by the misdeeds that arise from our sinful flesh. How is this resolved? In one word — confession. As we believers bring our guilty consciences to Christ, acknowledge our wrongdoing, and agree with Him that what we've done is unacceptable, Christ is faithful to continually remove our sin and guilt (1 John 1:9).

Guilt is relieved in Christ. Often because of

our past or because we are especially desirous of pleasing our Lord, we "feel" a sense of guilt for something we might have done or might do. It isn't a reality, but we still feel guilty. How do we escape these gnawing accusations? If they are true, confess them. And if they are not true, thank Christ profusely for His unfailing love that has forgiven you and will continue to forgive you until you see Him face-to-face.

Doing Your Part

As we approach the end of this book, I'm sure you can see that we have not addressed every single worry under the sun. I don't know about you, but my "worry book" could fill volumes! The issue is not the number of our worries, but the One who can assist us with our worries — Jesus. He is the One who communicated to us about worry in simple and easy-to-understand language: "Do not worry." Why is refusing to worry and breaking the worry habit God's plan for lasting peace of mind? Because there's no reason to ever worry. The God of the universe promises to be there with and for us, no matter where our path takes us. He promises to provide all our needs. He promises to keep us and protect us.

He promises to comfort and strengthen us. He promises to assist and help us. And He promises us a forever-home in heaven.

So why worry about the things we can't control? If we are going to worry about anything, it should be about the things that we can control — like the decisions we make and doing what's right.

✓ *Make it a habit to grow spiritually.* The apostle Paul had serious, multiple reasons to live his entire life under a black cloud of guilt for atrocious sins. Yet he is the one who tells us a secret: "Put on the whole armor of God, that you may be able to stand against the wiles of the devil" (Ephesians 6:11). The more you grow spiritually —

- the more you are aware of your problems with temptation and sin
- the more you know about God's gracious and forever forgiveness through Christ
- the more you know about God and His oversight and care of you, His sheep
- the more you know about God's goals for you as one of His children
- the more you can serve others as

you develop your spiritual giftedness
- the more you know about the enemy
and the need for the whole armor
God provides for you for the battle.

✓ *Make it a habit to continually confess
your sin.* As Jim constantly reminds me
— and now I'm reminding you again —
keep a short account with God. When
you sin, rush to confess it. You can do
it in a split second. Just say, "Oh, Lord,
that was so wrong! Forgive me." Refuse to let your fellowship with God,
your heavenly Father, be interrupted (1
John 1:9).

✓ *Make it a habit to avoid sinful situations.*
Choose to steer clear of any situation
that may cause you to sin (2 Timothy 2:22). Be aware of the effects of
your surroundings. You are a product
of your environment, which includes
people and places. If there are people
in your regular path who tempt you
away from the things of God, choose
to avoid them and choose other friends.
Remember, "evil company corrupts
good habits" (1 Corinthians 15:33).

And how about those places? I once read about a man who wanted to break his habit of eating ice cream every day. Yet he failed week after week. Finally he realized that if he altered his driving route home from work — which passed right by his favorite ice cream haunt — he didn't eat ice cream!

In my studies I discovered these final thoughts that I want to pass on to you as you recognize the importance of breaking bad habits: "Guilt is remorse and awareness that you've done something wrong. God forgives you when you confess and repent, but the feelings of guilt may linger. Instead of berating yourself for having these feelings, use them for positive action. Change your habits that lead to sin."[2]

Breaking the Worry Habit . . . Forever!

I hope and pray you are seeing worry for what it is — a bad habit that can and must be broken. Can't you just imagine a life without worry? Don't you desire the health and peace of mind and body a worry-free life would bring? Don't you yearn for burden-free days as you trust God, turn over every worry to

Him, and concentrate instead on doing your part? Don't you dream of possessing the energy to focus on serving others, the energy your fretting and anxiety is using up? You can have all of the above and be completely free to serve God with all your heart and truly enjoy peace of mind as you aim each day to break your worry habit. Look to God day by day. He is ready, willing, and able to help you with this all-important goal.

Let us therefore come boldly
to the throne of grace,
that we may obtain mercy and
find grace to help in time of need.
HEBREWS 4:16

Digging Deeper

QUESTIONS AND INSIGHTS TO HELP YOU BREAK THE WORRY HABIT

1
WHAT'S WRONG WITH ME?

1. When it comes to our physical health, medical news can be alarming. I shared about my cancer scare, and now it's your turn. Jot down any upsetting health issues you've experienced.

2. Share briefly how you coped with your health problem:

   • physically —

   • mentally —

- emotionally —

- spiritually —

3. Looking back, what might you do differently in a similar situation today?

4. What words of instruction, exhortation, encouragement, comfort, and hope would you give to women who are encountering health problems?

THE VAST SCOPE OF WORRIES

5. Have you heard the adage, "A problem defined is a problem half-solved"? List your primary concerns and areas of worry. Be honest. This list will help you understand the scope of your concerns.

6. List any health issues you're facing right now. If there aren't any, thank God profusely for your good health. What a blessing!

   • "The moment you're born, you begin to die." What do you think of this axiom?

7. How do the following scriptures affect your perspective on your life?

   • Isaiah 40:6–8 —

   • Philippians 1:21–23 —

8. *Good health is natural and normal.* Whatever your health situation is, how should you respond to God? (See Philippians 4:11–13.)

9. *We are not guaranteed a life free of pain or illness.* Do you agree or disagree with this statement? Why?

- Read Colossians 1:9–11. Why do you think Paul was more concerned for our spiritual condition than our physical condition?

10. *Physical pain isn't necessarily bad.* Write about a time when you or someone you know sought medical help early because of pain or physical symptoms. What was the outcome?

11. *Physical pain is an opportunity to trust God.* Look up Matthew 26:39–44. What was Jesus' desire as He faced His upcoming pain and suffering?

- Now look at 2 Corinthians 1:3–5. Describe how your experience with suffering can benefit others.

12. *Spiritual health is more important than physical health.* According to Philippians 3:20–21, how should you view your present physical situation?

- Paul asked people to pray for spiritual matters, which is what his Lord and Savior, Jesus, did. Scan through John 17. Then note the spiritual matters Jesus prayed for concerning His followers as seen in these verses:

  - Verse 15 —

  - Verses 17 and 19 —

  - Verse 21 —

- Read Ephesians 1:15–19. List some of Paul's additional prayer concerns for his readers at Ephesus.

_____

Doing Your Part

13. What steps can you take in each of these areas to do your part in taking care of your health? List at least one step for each item.

- Watch over your body —

- Watch what you eat —

- Watch your weight —

- Exercise regularly —

- Have regular checkups —

- Follow up on warning signs —

- Keep your focus on heaven —

- Trust in the providence of God —

Breaking the Worry Habit . . . Forever!

14. Read this section in your book again. What insights did you gain from this section . . . and the entire chapter . . . regarding worrying about your health?

15. How do you think breaking your habit of worrying about your health and choosing to trust God will contribute to greater peace of mind?

16. As you think about the seriousness of your worry habit and some ways to

break it, what specific steps will you take to enjoy greater peace of mind?

❧ Today I will . . .

❧ This week I will . . .

❧ In the future I will . . .

2
MORE MONTH THAN MONEY

Digging Deeper

1. Read again Sue's story about her concerns regarding her family's financial condition. What areas of her story can you identify with? Also jot down any additional concerns you have about finances.

2. Share briefly how you generally cope with problems regarding money matters:

   • physically —

   • mentally —

- emotionally —

- spiritually —

3. What words of instruction, exhortation, encouragement, comfort, and hope would you give to Sue and others who are dealing with money challenges?

FACING A FEW FACTS ABOUT FINANCES

4. Money, along with its use and misuse, is addressed often in the Bible. Financial problems aren't a recent invention or problem. For many women today, money seems to be a top concern. What do these verses say about the effects of money?

- What happened when a couple allowed money to influence their relationship with God in Acts 5:1–10?

- What is one common qualification for church leadership?

  - 1 Timothy 3:3 —

  - 1 Timothy 3:8 —

  - Titus 1:7 —

- Why do you think the way a person views and uses money is an important qualification for leadership?

- Describe what happens when people want to "get rich" and why, according to 1 Timothy 6:9–10.

- In the last days, what will be the general attitude toward money (2 Timothy 3:2)? (The last days are the period between the writing of this second letter to Timothy and the second coming of Jesus. You're living in the "last days"!)

"Do Not Worry"

5. Once again, consider Jesus' command in Matthew 6:25. He made it clear we shouldn't worry. How do these verses reinforce His teachings?

- Isaiah 26:3 —

- Isaiah 41:10 and 13 —

- Jeremiah 17:8–9 —

- Matthew 10:25–31 —

- Luke 12:11 —

- John 14:1–3 —

COUNTING ON GOD

6. Look at these verses in your Bible and jot down a few words regarding their message about God's provision for the needs of His people.

  - 2 Corinthians 9:10–11 —

  - Philippians 4:19 —

7. One more time, read through Matthew 6:25–34 and make a few notes about how this passage encourages you to trust God for all aspects of your life, including your finances.

8. To ensure that finances won't become a source of worry for you, describe how you will implement these strategies this week.

   - Keep your head and your heart in God's Word —

   - Get help. Seek financial help from people you trust and who love God —

   - Pray about how you handle finances —

9. How can the advice in these scriptures help decrease your worries about finances . . . and anything else?

   - 2 Corinthians 9:8 —

   - Ephesians 3:20 —

• Philippians 4:13 —

10. When it comes to work, how can Colossians 3:24 help you . . .

   • work hard? —

   • cut back? —

   • talk with your children? —

   • do your part . . . in spite of others? —

TAPPING INTO GOD'S PEACE

11. How does Philippians 4:11–13 give you peace of mind when it comes to finances?

   • How is contentment learned?

- How should salvation through Christ teach us to be content?

- How can circumstances teach us to be content?

- How do trials teach us to be content?

12. What is a key element in doing what must be done, according to 2 Corinthians 12:9?

Breaking the Worry Habit . . . Forever!

13. Read this section in your book again. What insights did you gain from this section . . . and the entire chapter . . . regarding worrying about your finances?

14. How do you think breaking your habit of worrying about your finances and choosing to trust God will contribute to greater peace of mind?

15. As you think about the seriousness of your worry habit and some ways to break it, what specific steps will you take to enjoy greater peace of mind?

    ✣ Today I will . . .

    ✣ This week I will . . .

    ✣ In the future I will . . .

3
'TIL DEATH DO US PART

Digging Deeper

1. If you're married, what areas of Gladys' story do you identify with? Also note any other areas of concern you have.

2. Share briefly how you generally cope with problems regarding your husband:

   • mentally —

   • emotionally —

- spiritually —

3. What words of instruction, exhortation, encouragement, comfort, and hope would you give to Gladys and other wives who are dealing with marital challenges?

Worry for Your Husband

4. If you're married, consider these areas of concern for your husband. Note your fears and realities under each area. Then pause and pray about each one. Determine what is out of your control and what you can do to help.

- Health issues —

- Job issues —

- Spiritual issues —

- Fidelity issues —

- Friendship issues —

What's a Wife to Do?

5. Quickly read Abigail's story in 1 Samuel 25.

- What was David's request (verses 1–9)?

- How did Nabal respond to David's request (verses 10–12)?

- What was David's response (verse 13)?

6. A servant came to Abigail with details of the conversation Nabal had with David's men. What was the justification

for David's request for supplies from Nabal (verses 14–16)?

- According to the report from the servant, what was David about to do (verse 17)?

- What actions did Abigail take to defuse the potential crisis (verses 18–20)?

- What was Abigail's appeal to David (verses 23–31)?

- After Abigail's appeal, what was David's assessment of her (verses 32–33)?

- What was the outcome of Abigail's intervention (verses 34–35)?

7. List two or three key lessons you learn from Abigail about how you can help your husband.

8. What do these verses teach you about what to do . . . and not do . . . as a wife to promote harmony in your marriage?

- Proverbs 12:4 —

- Proverbs 14:1 —

- Proverbs 19:13–14 —

- Proverbs 21:9 and 19 —

- Proverbs 27:15–16 —

- 1 Peter 3:1–2 —

- What is the bottom-line message of these verses?

- Which principle needs your attention right away . . . today?

Doing Your Part

9. Since marriage is a team effort, what steps can you take in these areas to do your part in your marriage? Note several in each area.

- Stop worrying about your husband's faults —

- Step up your prayers for your husband —

- Talk to your husband —

Breaking the Worry Habit . . . Forever!

10. Read this section in your book again. What insights did you gain from this section . . . and the entire chapter . . . regarding worrying about your husband?

11. How do you think breaking your habit of worrying about your husband and choosing to trust God will contribute to greater peace of mind?

12. As you think about the seriousness of your worry habit and some ways to break it, what specific steps will you take to enjoy greater peace of mind?

🌿 Today I will . . .

🌿 This week I will . . .

🌿 In the future I will . . .

4

DO YOU KNOW WHERE YOUR CHILDREN ARE?

Digging Deeper

1. Read Pam's story about her family again. If you have children, what areas of her story do you identify with? If you have other areas of parenting concerns, jot them down too.

2. Share briefly how you generally cope with parenting problems:

   • mentally —

   • emotionally —

• spiritually —

3. What words of instruction, exhortation, encouragement, comfort, and hope would you give Pam and other moms who are dealing with child-raising challenges?

MOMS LOVE TO WORRY ABOUT DANGER
4. Read Hagar's story in Genesis 21:1–21.

• What was the purpose of the feast (verse 8)?

• What happened at this feast (verse 9)?

• What was Sarah's reaction (verses 10–11)?

- What was Abraham's response to Sarah's demands (verses 12–14)?

- What reassurance did God give concerning Hagar and her son?

- What were Hagar's fears as she and her son wandered in the desert (verses 15–16)?

- How did God demonstrate His faithfulness to Hagar and her son (verses 17–21)?

5. If you're a mom (and grandmom), what concerns do you have for your children and grandchildren?

- How does God's treatment of Hagar and her son reassure you for your children and grandchildren?

MOMS LOVE TO WORRY ABOUT SUCCESS

6. Scan the full story of Rebekah and her ambitions for Jacob in Genesis 27:1–45.

   - What prompted Rebekah's actions (verses 1–4)?

   - What was Rebekah's plan (verses 5–10)?

   - How did Jacob react to his mother's scheme (verses 11–12)?

- How did Rebekah respond and act (verses 13–17)?

- What was the immediate result of the deception (verses 27–29)?

- What was the long-term and tragic result of Rebekah's manipulation of the family situation (verses 41–45)?

7. All of this worry and conniving by Rebekah could have been avoided if she'd believed God. What was His promise to her while the twins were still in her womb (Genesis 25:23)?

- What do you learn about worrying for your children and their success from Rebekah's story? (See Matthew 6:33.)

8. Timothy grew spiritually and eventually became a valued member of Paul's missionary team. What insights do you gain from Timothy's early training as a child and youth from these verses?

- 2 Timothy 1:5 —

- 2 Timothy 3:14–15 —

- How do these elements in Timothy's maturing process challenge you in your role in the spiritual growth of your children?

9. A bonus! Let's look at three moms whose children grew spiritually to the point they were hugely successful in their service for God and His people. We can be sure these moms were tempted to worry as their children left the nest for ministry. As you read

each mother/child story, jot down any evidence that the mothers worried. Remember that communication in those days was infrequent and limited.

- Read 1 Samuel 1 and 2:1–10. Hannah delivered her three-year-old son, Samuel, to the priest to be raised in the temple to serve God. As you read 1 Samuel 1:10 and 2:1–10, did you note one of Hannah's weapons against worry? What was it?

- Read Luke 2:39–52. What evidence do you find about Mary worrying about her son, Jesus?

- We know that at about age 30, Jesus officially entered into the active fulfillment of His ministry on earth. His work and lifestyle eventually had Mary watching her precious Son being crucified on a cross (John 19:25). If you were Mary, what worries would you have talked to God about during Jesus' ministry and the days leading up to His death?

- Review what you learned about Timothy and his usefulness to the apostle Paul (see question 8). Now read Acts 16:1–11. If you were Timothy's mother, Eunice, what worries would you have to give to God as your young adult son left home to travel the world, which was largely unknown at the time?

- How will these examples of moms and their children encourage you when your kids are away, whether at a sleepover, church camp, college, on a mission field, or living far away (single or married)?

Doing Your Part

10. Do you worry excessively about and for your children? What did you learn in the first paragraph regarding your challenges and your peace of mind? How will this help you?

11. *Pray for your children.* What steps can you take to be more consistent in praying for your children?

12. *Be available to your children.* How can you free up your schedule so you will be more available to your kids?

13. *Prepare your children.* List the steps you're already taking to protect your children from the world.

   • What other steps will you take?

14. *Guard your children.* Protecting your children is a parent's offensive weapon. Guarding your children is a defensive tactic. What are you doing to guard them from the world?

 • What more needs to be done?

15. There are physical and spiritual battles being waged around your children. Write out a statement of your resolve to pray, protect, and guard your children.

Breaking the Worry Habit . . . Forever!

16. Read this section in your book again. What insights did you gain from this section . . . and the entire chapter . . . regarding worrying about your children?

17. How do you think breaking your habit of worrying about your children and choosing to trust God will contribute to greater peace of mind?

18. As you think about the seriousness of your worry habit and some ways to break it, what specific steps will you take to enjoy greater peace of mind?

   ✎ Today I will . . .

   ✎ This week I will . . .

   ✎ In the future I will . . .

5
I'M 30 AND STILL SINGLE!

Digging Deeper

1. If you're single, what areas of Claire's story do you identify with? Also jot down any other areas of concern you have.

2. If you're married, what are some thoughts and emotions you experienced while you were single?

3. Share briefly how you cope (or coped) with your singleness:

   • physically —

- mentally —

- emotionally —

- spiritually —

- socially —

4. What words of instruction, exhortation, encouragement, and comfort would you give to Claire and other single women who are distressed by their situation?

5. This section could also be called "God's Perspective on Marriage" because marriage and singleness are two sides of the same coin. They both involve knowing and submitting to God's perfect will. Because this is such an important message for all women, let's dig a little deeper. Scan 1 Corinthians 7:1–40.

- Basically the Corinthians asked Paul, "Is it better to be married than not to be married?" What are two advantages of being married (verses 2, 7, and 9)?

- What are the advantages of remaining single according to:

  - Paul's perspective (verses 1, 6, and 7–8)? —

  - Paul's observation on singleness (verses 32–35)? —

- After hearing these two sides of marriage versus singleness, you might ask, "Which state is better?" Paul teaches that each believer will find the answer if he or she understands what three factors involving God?

  - Factor 1 (verse 17) —

  - Factor 2 (verse 19) —

  - Factor 3 (verses 20–24, especially 23) —

SINGLES AND SERVICE

6. If a woman like Claire, with her worries about her singleness, came to you, how would you encourage her focus after reading and studying 1 Corinthians 7?

7. Jot down a few facts about these single women and their service to Jesus and to the early church.

- Mary Magdalene

  - Matthew 28:1, 7–8 —

  - Mark 15:40–41 —

  - Luke 8:2–3 —

  - John 19:25 —

  - John 20:1–2 —

  - John 20:11–18 —

- Mary and Martha

  - Luke 10:38–42 —

  - John 12:2–3, 7 —

- Phoebe

  - Romans 16:1–2 —

WIDOWS AND WORRY

8. Why do you think the Bible offers so many illustrations of women who were widowed and gives such a significant number of verses associated with widows?

- How does the topic of "widows and worry" apply to you as a woman?

9. You read in your book that "a widow can completely count on God for all her needs." In addition to the verses in your book, look up these scriptures and share how they encourage every woman who is a widow and every woman who may one day be a widow.

A widow can count on God for her care.

- Even as the Israelites were on their way to the promised land, what was one of God's concerns (Exodus 22:22–24)?

- Proverbs 15:25 —

- Jeremiah 49:11 —

- James 1:27 —

A widow can count on God's people for care.

- According to Acts 6:1–3, how did taking care of the widows begin in the early church?

WIDOWS AND SERVICE

10. Review these Bible passages and verses, which describe the ministries and service of the most prominent widows in the Bible. What was significant about the service of each of these widows, and how does it inspire you to greater service to your family, your church, and your community?

- Ruth (Ruth 2) —

- The widow of Zarephath (1 Kings 17:9–16) —

- Anna (Luke 2:37) —

- The widow who gave all (Mark 12:42) —

- A group of modern-day servants —

  * Describe some widows you know who faithfully serve others. Then pray for them.

Doing Your Part

11. Read this section in your book again. How can you encourage your single friends in each of these areas? If you're single, what can you do in each area?

- Embrace your singleness —

- Own your role —

- Keep yourself pure —

- Encourage those who are single —

Breaking the Worry Habit . . . Forever!

12. Read this section in your book again. What insights did you gain from this section . . . and the entire chapter . . . regarding worrying about singleness?

13. How do you think breaking your habit of worrying about singleness and choosing to trust God will contribute to greater peace of mind?

14. As you think about the seriousness of your worry habit and some ways to break it, what specific steps will you take to enjoy greater peace of mind?

⚘ Today I will . . .

⚘ This week I will . . .

⚘ In the future I will . . .

6
WHY DO I HAVE TO BE
THE RESPONSIBLE ONE?

Digging Deeper

1. Read Ann Marie's story about her many responsibilities. Make your own to-do list for tomorrow. (As long as you're taking the time to make the list, why not write it on a separate piece of paper so you can use it tomorrow?)

2. Share briefly how you generally cope with your daily and on-going list of responsibilities:

   • physically —

- mentally —

- emotionally —

- spiritually —

3. What words of instruction, exhortation, encouragement, comfort, and hope would you give to Ann Marie and other busy women who are struggling with the weight of their many responsibilities?

THE BURDEN OF RESPONSIBILITY

4. List and describe your normal, everyday duties and responsibilities. Also identify the time in the course of your day when you often feel that successfully managing your life is impossible.

5. Jesus was by far the most important houseguest ever. How did these two sisters handle His visit to their home (Luke 10:38–40)?

- Mary —

- Martha —

- What do you learn from each sister about the way you are — or could be — handling your responsibilities?

    * From Mary —

    * From Martha —

- Write out Luke 10:41–42, using *your* name instead of Martha's. When you're finished, write your thoughts on how Jesus' words can apply to your priorities.

6. Martha is a perfect example of getting so involved in a project that she loses sight of the many reasons why she decided to do a project in the first place. Recall a time when you were a "Martha" while fulfilling a responsibility at home or at work or church. Note the details and how your actions compare with Martha's.

- Martha became obsessed —

- Martha became rude —

- Martha became bossy —

JESUS UNDERSTANDS!

7. Read through Luke 10:38–42 again. Who did Jesus point Martha to as an example . . . and why?

8. You have the same two options when it comes to your work, responsibilities, and service. You can go Martha's way or you can go Mary's way. For a visual aid, write out the two options:

- Martha's choice —

- Mary's choice —

  * How did Mary's choice bring about peace of mind?

Doing Your Part

9. As you review this section in your book, describe how each of the to-do list suggestions can help you handle frustration and worry. Write out what you can do as your part, and what you can change in your lifestyle to handle these areas better. Remember Jesus' command: "Do not worry."

- Revisit your priorities —

- Re-examine your service —

- Revise your schedule —

- Reap the blessings —

Breaking the Worry Habit . . . Forever!

10. Read this section in your book again. What insights did you gain from this section . . . and the entire chapter . . . regarding worrying about your responsibilities?

11. How do you think breaking your habit of worrying about your responsibilities and choosing to trust God will contribute to greater peace of mind?

12. As you think about the seriousness of your worry habit and some ways to break it, what specific steps will you take to enjoy greater peace of mind?

✂ Today I will . . .

✂ This week I will . . .

✂ In the future I will . . .

7

Be Careful with That!

1. Read Sue's story relating her fears and worries about possessions. What areas in her story do you identify with? Also jot down any other worries you have in this area.

2. Share briefly how you generally cope with your desires, thoughts, and re-actions when it comes to the things you own — or would like to own:

   • mentally —

   • emotionally —

- physically —

- spiritually —

A Personal Confession

3. We witnessed some of the results of Sue's desire for the "right" home in the "right" neighborhood, with the "right" furnishings. I've also shared some of my own struggles with wanting more. Living with contentment in this world is definitely a struggle. That's why the Bible warns us, "Do not love the world or the things in the world" (1 John 2:15). Describe any struggles you've had or are having now with assigning possessions a higher priority than they should have.

Putting Possessions into a Proper Perspective

Jesus often spoke about the importance of the focus of our time, money, and possessions.

4. *Possessions can divide your allegiance to God.* Jesus says there are two ways of viewing life, your possessions, and even where you spend your time and concentrate your attention. According to Matthew 6:19, where are most people tempted to place their focus?

- What does Jesus say can happen to your treasure and goods when you choose this option?

- Share about a time when you experienced this reality, such as a piece of clothing ruined or throwing out some food items.

5. According to verse 20, where does Jesus say you should place your focus?

- What happens to your treasure when you choose this option?

- Why is your choice so important, and what does it reveal?

    * Verse 21 —

    * Verse 24 —

- James picks up on this truth in James 4:4. What does he have to say about choices?

6. Now read 1 John 2:15–17 and put the messages into your own words:

    - Verse 15 —

- Verse 16 —

- Verse 17 —

7. Look again at verse 16. What three lusts, or cravings, or covetous desires should you be on guard against?

  •

  •

  •

8. *Possessions don't last.* What do you learn about the transitory nature of possessions in 2 Peter 3:10?

- Rather than focusing on earthly possessions that will not last, where should your focus be instead, according to:

- 2 Peter 3:11 —

- 2 Peter 3:13 —

9. *Possessions are a stewardship.* Read through Matthew 25:14–30. How do you rate yourself as a steward of God's possessions? In your opinion, should God give you more to take care of . . . or take away what He's already given to you? Why?

- What changes in attitude and practice do you need to make to become a more faithful steward?

10. *Possessions do not equal contentment.* Proverbs 30:7–9 describes how con-

tentment works. What does verse 8 say our desires should be?

- What can happen when we have too much (verse 9)?

- And when we have too little?

11. *Possessions are not the end goal.* Think about your lifetime goals. Do any of them involve wealth or a comfortable home with everything you think you need? Do you need to alter your end goals . . . or how you're planning for the future?

12. *Possessions do not satisfy.* What does? What do these verses say about being truly blessed?

- Ecclesiastes 2:11 —

- Isaiah 58:10–11 —

- Proverbs 22:9 —

- According to Psalm 91:1 and 15–16, who is blessed, and how is he blessed?

HOLDING YOUR POSSESSIONS LIGHTLY

13. Have you heard the expression, "You are blessed to be a blessing"? Note these instances of blessing others. What do they say you can do to bless others?

- Luke 3:11 —

- Galatians 6:10 —

- James 2:14–17 —

14. Scan again through the accounts in the book of the people in the Bible who gave generously. Choose one and share how that person motivates and inspires you to be more aware of the needs of those around you. As a super bonus to yourself, do this for all of these saints who held their possessions lightly and knew God was the provider of all they had.

- *Heart question:* What do you own that you could not give away or share with someone else? Why? Do you need to reconsider your attitude?

15. What steps can you take in each of the following areas to do your part in lining up your perspective on possessions with God's?

- Embrace a heavenly perspective —

- Evaluate what you have —

- Enumerate what you are willing to give away —

- Examine what you want —

- Enjoy freedom from worry —

16. Read this section in your book again. What insights did you gain from this section . . . and the entire chapter . . . regarding worrying about your possessions . . . or lack of them?

17. How do you think breaking your habit of worrying about your responsibilities and choosing to trust God will contribute to greater peace of mind?

18. As you think about the seriousness of your worry habit and some ways to break it, what specific steps will you take to enjoy greater peace of mind?

    ✌ Today I will . . .

    ✌ This week I will . . .

    ✌ In the future I will . . .

8
I DON'T WANT TO GO!

1. Read Rita's story again. What areas of her story can you identify with? Also jot down any other personal fears you experience.

2. Share briefly how you generally cope with your fears and anxieties about potentially harmful situations:

   • physically —

   • mentally —

- emotionally —

- spiritually —

3. What words of instruction, exhortation, encouragement, comfort, and hope would you give to Rita and others who are caught in crippling fears?

Worrying About the "What Ifs"

4. Queen Esther is a prime example of a woman who got caught up in worrying about "what ifs." The evil Haman had persuaded the king to send out an edict to have all the Jews killed on a specific date. Read Esther 4:1–17.

- How did Mordecai (Esther's older cousin) respond to the news of the plot against the Jews (verses 1–4)?

- How did Queen Esther show her concern for Mordecai as he sat in the gate mourning over the evil plan (verse 4)?

- What information was related back to Esther (verses 5–7)?

- What did Mordecai request of Esther (verses 8–9)?

- What was Esther's initial "what if" response (verses 10–11)?

- How did Mordecai respond to her fears (verses 12–14)?

- Once Esther reflected on her unique position as queen, what request did she make of the Jews in Susa (verses 15–16)?

- Esther went from "what if" to "why not." What famous statement of faith did she proclaim, as noted in verse 16?

"WHERE IS YOUR FAITH?"

5. Read Luke 8:22–25.

- What was Jesus' plan (verse 22)?

- What crisis arose, and how severe was it (verse 23)?

- What was Jesus doing (verse 23)?

- How did the disciples respond — or react! — to the crisis (verse 24)?

- What was Jesus' response to their fear?

  - In verse 24 —

  - In verse 25 —

- Once again, what was Jesus' plan (verse 22)?

- The disciples failed this test of faith because they didn't latch onto Jesus' plan that He was going to the other side, which meant *they* were going to the other side with Him, which meant they would reach the shore. What does this teach you about answering the question "Where is your faith?" when you're in the midst of storms?

FAITH FIGHTS FEAR AND WORRY

Before we move on, remember how the disciples acted. They looked around and saw danger. They looked within and saw fear. They failed to look up with trust and acknowledge God or look to Jesus and trust Him.

6. *Trust exhibits courage.* Read Exodus 14:13–14 for yourself in your Bible.

   • What was Moses' initial exhortation to the fearful people?

   • What did he advise them to do instead of disintegrating into fear?

315

- So much for the people's part. Now for God's part! What did Moses have to say about God's involvement in the care of the people?

- Note several lessons you learn from this story about fear and courage.

7. Read Daniel 3:14–30. All the people were commanded to worship a statue of the king.

   - What was the consequence of failing to do so (verse 15)?

   - How did Daniel's three friends communicate and model trust in God (verses 16–18)?

   - What was the exciting outcome of their faith and courage in the fire (verses 26–29)?

- Note several lessons you learn from this story about fear and courage.

8. *Trust manifests confidence.* In another scenario, Peter's trust was short-lived as he stepped out in faith to walk on the water to Jesus. Cowered by the effects of the wind, his faith faltered (Matthew 14:30). His faith was also nonexistent in the courtyard after Jesus was betrayed by Judas (Matthew 26:69–75). But after the coming of the Holy Spirit, Peter changed.

- Read Acts 4:5–20. How did Peter and John exhibit courage and confidence before the intimidating council of Jewish leaders?

9. *Trust demonstrates belief.* Read Genesis 15:1–6, which occurs right after Abraham (referred to as Abram) defeated the kings of the East. Perhaps Abra-

ham was worrying, "Will there be a reprisal?"

- What was God's command to Abraham in a vision? And what did God say about Himself (verse 1)?

- Once God initiated this conversation with Abraham, what did Abraham request of God (verses 2–3)?

- After hearing Abraham's concerns, what was God's promise to Abraham (verses 4–5)?

- What was Abraham's heart response (verse 6)?

- Check out verse 1 again. Do you believe God is able to handle your problems?

  * What anxieties do you need to talk over with Him? When will you do this?

10. *Trust models patience.* Read Genesis 16:1–6, and describe a time when you, like Sarah (referred to as Sarai), became impatient with God's timing and took matters into your own hands. What did you do, and what was the result?

  - Now scan Luke 1:5–7. How did Elizabeth model patience?

    * Think about a problem you're facing. What can you take away from Elizabeth's godly example?

11. *Trust displays obedience.* Trust and obedience for Abraham — and the Israelites, Daniel's three friends, and Peter, John, and Elizabeth — were on-going exercises in faith.

- Do you believe that each new day and each new challenge are opportunities for you to demonstrate your trust by obedience? How do you feel about that?

- When facing a new day or challenge, what will your first step be?

Doing Your Part

Exercising your physical muscles requires a lot of effort. Growing closer in your walk with Jesus also involves work. You have to do your part.

12. *Build a close relationship with Christ.*
    Read Galatians 5:16–26. If you "walk
    in the Spirit," what will happen (verse
    16)?

    • Verse 17 informs us there will be a
      fierce struggle within each believer.
      Who — or what — are the two ri-
      vals in this struggle?

    • The flesh and the Spirit each ex-
      hibit their unique manifestations or
      nature. What does walking in the
      flesh look like (verses 19–21)?

    • By contrast, what does walking in
      the Spirit look like (verses 22–23)?

    • What do you learn in verses 24–26
      that will motivate you to want to

walk in the Spirit instead of the flesh?

- To draw closer to Jesus, list at least one or two changes you can make in these two vital growth areas:

  • reading the Bible —

  • praying for God's guidance —

13. *Build up your trust in Christ.* Peter's growth in trust is an encouragement to you and me . . . regarding all the "what ifs" we think of. Look up these "growth" verses and note how they will help you.

   - Psalm 56:3 —

   - Psalm 56:11 —

322

- Philippians 1:21 —

- Philippians 4:6–7 —

- Philippians 4:8 —

Breaking the Worry Habit . . . Forever!

14. Read this section in your book again. What insights did you gain from this section . . . and the entire chapter . . . regarding worrying about potential fears and future problems?

15. How do you think breaking your habit of worrying about "what ifs" and choosing to trust God will contribute to greater peace of mind?

16. As you think about the seriousness of your worry habit and some ways to break it, what specific steps will you take to enjoy greater peace of mind?

- Today I will . . .

- This week I will . . .

- In the future I will . . .

9
WHAT GOES AROUND COMES AROUND

Digging Deeper

1. Read again Betty's story about her many worries regarding her parents. What areas of her story do you identify with? Also note any other areas of concern you have.

2. Share briefly how you generally cope with your fears and anxieties about your parents:

   • physically —

   • mentally —

- emotionally —

- spiritually —

3. What words of instruction, exhortation, encouragement, comfort, and hope would you give to Betty and other women today who are worrying about their parents' health and welfare?

WORRYING ABOUT YOUR LIFESTYLE

4. Betty experienced a reality check, and it's time for your checkup as well. Take a few minutes to think about your lifestyle and how things are going. Jot down brief comments about your relationship with your parents, your busyness, your family life, your commitments, and your daily schedule. Where do your mom and dad fit in?

5. The apostle Paul wrote to the believers in Galatia to help them understand what a Spirit-filled family looks like. And it all starts with Spirit-filled individuals.

- What does a Spirit-filled person look like, according to Galatians 5:22–23?

- How do Spirit-filled children of any age act around their parents (Ephesians 6:1–2)?

- What suggestions would you give to another woman about how a busy wife and mom can — and should — appreciate her parents?

HONOR YOUR PARENTS

6. Honoring your parents is high on God's list of important activities, and this

goes way beyond mere appreciation. To experience the power and importance of this command, which is one of the Ten Commandments in the Old Testament, read Exodus 19:16–20; 20:1–20.

- Describe the physical setting (19:16–20).

- How significant and fearsome do you think it was for a man to "talk" with God, and for God to "talk" with a man in this way?

- What was the fifth commandment God told Moses (Exodus 20:12)?

- Read Leviticus 20:1, 9. What was God's command here?

- Read Deuteronomy 27:11, 16. For what would the people be cursed?

- Obviously God cares how we treat our parents, so it should be no surprise that He continues this message in the New Testament. Who is talking and what is being said in these passages?

  - Matthew 15:1–9 (see also Mark 7:6–13) —

  - Matthew 19:16–19 —

- According to 1 Timothy 5:4, what are you to do regarding your parents?

- How can you honor and show your appreciation for your parents today? This week? In the future? Jot down a few thoughts. (And include your parents-in-law too!)

PUTTING LOVE INTO ACTION

7. One fruit of the Spirit is love (Galatians 5:22). After reading this section in your book, you probably agree that Ruth is an excellent model of loving and honoring her mother-in-law. Scan this section in your book again (and, if you have time, the book of Ruth). It's one thing to watch Ruth's love in action. Now it's time for you to turn up the love dial. Describe how you've demonstrated love to your parents (and parents-in-law if you're married):

- *Ruth left all to help her mother-in-law.* What was the latest sacrifice you made for your parents? For your in-laws? Do your parents and/or in-laws need anything that you're hesitating about because of the sacrifice required?

- *Ruth showed authentic devotion.* How are you demonstrating devotion to your parents on a regular basis? To your in-laws?

- *Ruth served her mother-in-law.* What acts of service have you recently performed for your parents? How can you do even more for them? And for your parents-in-law?

- *Ruth accepted advice.* Have your parents and/or in-laws offered any advice to you recently? If so, how did you respond to them and in your heart?

- *Ruth accepted help.* Are you a daughter who gives the impression of being self-sufficient so you don't need help or advice from your parents? Describe the last time you allowed your parents to help you.

- How can you get your parents more involved in your life and in the lives of your family members if you're married?

- Bonus question! How did Jesus demonstrate love for His mother even though He was experiencing extreme circumstances (John 19:25–27)?

Doing Your Part

8. Why not map out what you can do to honor your parents and your husband's parents? Add these to your daily planner and calendar so you'll follow through.

- *Plan to follow God's plan.* What can you do on a daily basis to honor and stay in touch with your mom and dad?

- *Plan to visit your parents.* Do you have a trip or a get-together in the works? Look at your calendar to see when a good time to visit will be. Invite them to your house or let them know you'll be coming to theirs (if they're available). If your parents live close to you, what are some activities you can do together this week?

- *Plan to call and write your parents often.* Read Proverbs 25:25. How can you cheer your parents' hearts? When will you call . . . and how often? And when . . . and how . . . will you write a letter, send a card, email, or text message? What "just because" gift can you send them this month?

- I will contact them . . .

- I will send them this gift . . .

- *Plan to pray for your parents.* If you pray daily, include your parents. Paul prayed for those he loved because he had them in his heart . . . or were they in his heart because he was praying for them? Either way, praying for your folks and in-laws (even when they're being difficult) helps fan your love for them and lifts them up to God. What specifically will you pray for them each day?

- *Plan to send pictures.* Although it may take a few extra minutes and extra money, your parents and grandparents will be truly pleased and blessed to get pictures of you and your family and friends. This also helps keep them up-to-date and involved. It's a great way to let them know you care.

- *Plan to seek your parents' advice.* What issues are coming up that you could ask for input on?

Breaking the Worry Habit . . . Forever!

9. Read this section in your book again. What insights did you gain from this section . . . and the entire chapter . . . regarding worrying about your parents?

10. How do you think breaking your habit of worrying about your parents and choosing to trust God will contribute to greater peace of mind?

11. As you think about the seriousness of your worry habit and some ways to break it, what specific steps will you take to enjoy greater peace of mind?

🌿 Today I will . . .

🌿 This week I will . . .

🌿 In the future I will . . .

10
WHAT WILL OTHERS THINK?

Digging Deeper

1. Read Lisa's story about her fears and worries about approval, rejection, and being alone and friendless. What areas do you identify with in her story? Also note any other anxieties you have in this area.

2. Share briefly how you generally cope with your problems and thoughts about the opinions of others:

   • mentally —

- emotionally —

- socially —

- spiritually —

3. What words of instruction, exhortation, encouragement, and hope would you give Lisa and other women who struggle with the age-old question, "What will others think?"

It's True Confession Time

4. We saw some of the results of Lisa's desire for approval. What are some of your weak spots when it comes to approval and acceptance? In what realms of performance, measuring up, clothing, or overall appearance are you concerned about what others will think?

5. Can you point to any negative effects these worries and concerns have had so far on your decisions or behavior, such as stifling your emotional health, social development, confidence, or willingness to step out for Christ?

WORRY AND THE APPROVAL OF OTHERS

6. Choose several of the people listed and read about their situations in your Bible. Write a sentence or two about their actions and any consequences. Also note why you picked them and their message to you about worrying about the approval of others. As a real bonus to yourself, do this for all of the Bible people in the list.

• Abraham (Genesis 12:10–20) —

• Isaac (Genesis 26:7–16) —

- King Saul (1 Samuel 13:1–17) —

- The Jewish leadership (John 11:45–53) —

- Pilate (Matthew 27:15–24; John 19:11–16) —

- The disciple Peter (Luke 22:54–62) —

- King Herod (Acts 12:1–4) —

- The apostle Peter (Galatians 2:11–16) —

7. About the failures of the Israelites, Paul wrote, "All these things happened to them as examples, and they were writ-

ten for our admonition" (1 Corinthians 10:11). As you think about the failures of these people, what messages are their examples sending to you across these many centuries? Or, put another way, what warnings and cautions about people-pleasing are you receiving from them as a whole?

IT'S A MATTER OF PRIORITIES

8. Not everyone caved in to the pressure to worry about approval. Some, like the following people, chose to desire the approval of God rather than people. Choose several and read about their situations. Write a sentence or two about their actions and any consequences. Also note why you picked them and their message to you about your worries regarding approval. Jot down why God should take first place in your life and in your choices. As a bonus, do this exercise for all the people listed. They set God and His will as their highest priority, which enabled them to stand firm in seeking God's approval regardless of personal suffering.

341

- Paul (Galatians 1:1–10) —

- Rahab (Joshua 2:1–14) —

- Daniel (Daniel 1:5–16) —

- The three friends of Daniel (3:13–30) —

- Peter and John (Acts 4:1–21) —

- Stephen (Acts 6:8–7:2, 51–60) —

9. Paul's words in 1 Corinthians 10:11 can also apply positively. When someone in the Bible does something sacrificial, noble, exemplary, we can be inspired and encouraged to follow in

their steps. As you think about the resolve of these people to remain faithful to God no matter what the cost, what messages are their examples sending to you across the centuries?

Doing Your Part

10. God loves you. You are His. Seek to please Him first rather than giving in and compromising just for the approval of people. You can turn a corner and resist the temptation. How? How will doing these key practices help you stay true to God?

- Keep your focus on God —

- See yourself as dead to self —

- Accept your eternal citizenship —

- Pray for personal boldness —

- Realize you are empowered by Christ —

Breaking the Worry Habit . . . Forever!

11. Read this section in your book again. What insights did you gain from this section . . . and the entire chapter . . . regarding worrying about the approval of others?

12. How do you think breaking your habit of worrying about pleasing people and choosing to trust God will contribute to greater peace of mind?

13. As you think about the seriousness of your worry habit and some ways to break it, what specific steps will you take to enjoy greater peace of mind?

❧ Today I will . . .

❧ This week I will . . .

❧ In the future I will . . .

11
WHAT IS THE RIGHT THING TO DO?

Digging Deeper

1. Read Anita's story about her fears and worries about making the right decisions. What areas in her story do you identify with? Also jot down any other worries you have in this area.

2. Share briefly how you generally cope with the opportunity — or necessity! — of making a decision about something or regarding someone in your life:

   • mentally —

- emotionally —

- physically —

- spiritually —

3. Looking back through time, what have you learned about decision making that guides you through the process today?

4. What words of instruction, exhortation, encouragement, comfort, and hope would you give to Anita and other women who are in the midst of making hard decisions?

5. Take a look at the Contents page to review some of the types of worry we've been labeling as bad. Share some of the common denominators that make them negative.

6. As you consider decision making, what could cause a worry to be categorized as good? What sets the worry in this chapter apart from the previous worries we've addressed?

DECISION-MAKING BLUNDERS
FROM THE BIBLE

Several men and women in the Bible made wrong decisions. Some should have known better, but they caved in to the pressure of their surroundings and took the easy road — the "safe" road. Look at each person in the following list and their decision.

7. *Eve.* Read Genesis 3:1–6 in your Bible. What was the progression of Eve's de-

cision-making process?

- Who did she consult before making her choice? Was her choice good or bad?

- What comments are made about Eve's decision in:

  * 2 Corinthians 11:3 —

  * 1 Timothy 2:13–14 —

- The consequences of Eve's choices were:

8. *Abraham.* At what point in the journey to Egypt did Abraham voice his worry about his own safety (Genesis 12:11–12)?

   • Describe a time when you were worried about something that *might* happen.

   • Did what you feared occur or were your worries unfounded? What happened?

   • What were the consequences or potential consequences of Abraham's choices?

9. *Lot.* Read Genesis 13:1–13. In your own words, describe the decision Lot was asked to make, and the choice he made. What was his decision based on, according to Genesis 13:10–11?

- Describe a time when you made a decision based on what looked good on the surface. What happened?

- The consequences of Lot's choice were:

10. *Moses.* What influenced both of Moses' decisions — to murder the Egyptian and strike the rock (Exodus 2:11–12; Numbers 20:9–11)?

- What was Moses' decision-making process? Who did he consult before acting?

- Describe a time when you made a decision based on instinctive feelings. What happened?

- The consequences of Moses' choices were:

11. *Orpah.* Quickly scan Ruth 1. Contrast the decisions made by the two daughters-in-law.

   - Orpah —

   - Ruth —

   - Can you think of a time when you were given a choice and took the easy road of staying in your comfort zone instead of the more risky road of following God? What happened?

12. *David.* After looking at 2 Samuel 12:2–4 in your Bible, list the progression of David's decisions that led to his sin

with Bathsheba, the wife of one of his warriors.

- *Bonus question:* Compare the decisions David made — or didn't make! — that led to his transgression with the many decisions Eve made that led to her decline into sin (Genesis 3:6). What similarities do you notice?

- *Extra bonus question:* Look at Joshua 7:21, Achan's confession regarding the decisions he made before stealing forbidden treasure. What choices led to breaking God's law?

- Take notes on the lessons you learn from David (and Eve and Achan) about the decisions that turned temptation into sin. Or note the decisions each failed to stop and make before moving headlong into sin.

13. Think about some of your most recent decisions, including your motives behind each one. Are there any patterns that are influencing your reasoning when you make your choices?

- Are you making it a habit to wait before deciding?

- Are you making it a habit to ask for advice before deciding?

- Are you making it a habit to pray before deciding?

Doing Your Part

14. As you're reading this chapter and answering these questions, what decisions

are you facing?

- What steps can you take in each of the areas below to assist you in making a right decision?

  - *Review each decision.* What happened when Ananias reviewed a decision he had to make in Acts 9:11–17?

  - *Refine your options.* How could praying Saul's (or Paul's) prayer in Acts 9:6 help you refine your options?

  - *Remember God's Word.* According to Joshua 1:8, how will remembering God's Word guide you . . . and bless you?

  - *Restrain your emotions.* This is possible when you walk by the Spirit. What fruits of the Spirit listed in Galatians 5:22–23 help you check your emotions? (And here's a bonus verse: Proverbs 16:32!)

• *Re-examine your motives.* How does Proverbs 3:6 help with the re-examination process?

• *Recount your resources.* What is your worst resource and your perfect resource according to Proverbs 3:5?

• *Resist impatience.* How does the principle in Proverbs 19:2 motivate you to be more thoughtful in making your decisions?

• *Respond and make the decision.* After all your planning, examining, reviewing, and refining, how do Proverbs 16:3 and 9 give you confidence when it's time to decide?

Breaking the Worry Habit . . . Forever!

15. Read this section in your book again. What insights did you gain from this section . . . and the entire chapter . . . regarding worrying about decision making?

16. How do you think breaking your habit of worrying about your responsibilities and choosing to trust God will contribute to greater peace of mind?

17. As you think about the seriousness of your worry habit and some ways to break it, what specific steps will you take to enjoy greater peace of mind?

Today I will . . .

✒ This week I will . . .

✒ In the future I will . . .

12
YOU CAN RUN,
BUT YOU CAN'T HIDE

Digging Deeper

1. Read Carol's story relating her fears and worries about guilt. What areas in the story of her worries and anxieties do you identify with? Also jot down any other worries you have in this area.

2. Share briefly how you generally cope with guilt and the conviction of sin:

   • mentally —

   • emotionally —

- physically —

- spiritually —

3. Looking back through time, what have you learned about taking care of guilt and settling it with God?

4. What words of instruction, exhortation, encouragement, comfort, and hope would you offer to Carol and other women who are living with guilt?

THANK GOD FOR A MORAL COMPASS!

5. Your book contains a list of references in the Bible referring to your conscience. Now it's time for you to see them for yourself. Look up these verses and write in your own words the key information about the conscience.

- Romans 2:1–15 —

- Hebrews 9:14 —

- Acts 24:16 —

- 1 Corinthians 8 —

- James 4:17 —

- Hebrews 13:18 —

- 1 Peter 3:16 —

6. Guilt is knowing you've done something wrong, and knowing something must be done to make it right. Guilt quickly becomes a reason for worry. But unless guilt leads to repentance, its only outcome is to make you feel miserable. Read Matthew 27:3–5 and describe how Judas felt about his guilt and how he dealt with it.

7. *Beware of temptation.* Realize that temptation is not sin. What are two ways to handle temptation according to 2 Timothy 2:22?

   •

   •

8. What did the wise, caring father tell his son about dealing with sin and tempta-

tion in Proverbs 4:25–27?

- Verse 25 —

- Verse 26 —

- Verse 27 —

9. To summarize these verses from 2 Timothy and Proverbs, note what you are not to do when you're tempted. Also write out what you are to do when tempted or to avoid temptation.

10. *Be aware of sin's consequences.* What is the warning in Hebrews 12:15?

- Share an example of a time when you made a selfish choice that hurt someone else.

- Also list those who are closest to you, the ones who have the greatest chance of being hurt by your wrong choices.

- How does the fact that "every sin is an act of total selfishness and yet it always harms someone else" make you want to refrain from sin?

11. *Be quick to acknowledge sin.* How do you think keeping a short record with God will dispel guilt?

- What time limit does Ephesians 4:26 establish for dealing with sin? Also what reason does verse 27 give for such speed?

- How does Psalm 51:4 motivate you to take care of all sin quickly?

12. *Be free!* We are a rebellious people. We can go for days, weeks, months, even years and decades without making things right with others and with God. Are you holding on to any sin — failing to acknowledge it, confess it, and be done with it? If so, you can take care of it now. Admit it to God right away and experience freedom from bondage. You can put a stop to any misery created by sin and guilt. You can also mend your alienation from God and those whom you have harmed. Take a look at these verses and jot down how God makes your freedom possible.

• Colossians 2:13 —

• Psalm 32:1–5 —

• Romans 8:2 —

• John 8:31–32, 36 —

"Jesus Paid It All"

13. Read this section describing what Jesus has done for you to take care of sin and guilt. If you are God's child — a Christian — then "Jesus paid it all" for you. Your burden of sin and guilt has been paid for and lifted from your heart. Look at these scriptures and note what God has done for you.

• Hebrews 10:1–10 —

• Matthew 26:28 —

• John 10:28 —

14. As His child, thank Him in prayer. Write a brief prayer of praise and

thanksgiving to Him for His grace given to you.

Doing Your Part

15. Habits can either be good or bad. Whenever you purposefully and regularly attempt any action that moves you in the direction of godliness, you are seeking to form a good habit. List several steps you can take in each of these areas that, by God's grace and with His help, will become godly habits.

- Make it a habit to grow spiritually —

- Make it a habit to continually confess your sin —

- Make it a habit to avoid sinful situations —

16. Read this section in your book again. What insights did you gain from this section . . . and the entire chapter . . . regarding worrying about your responsibilities?

17. How do you think breaking your habit of worrying about your responsibilities and choosing to trust God will contribute to greater peace of mind?

18. As you think about the seriousness of your worry habit and some ways to break it, what specific steps will you take to enjoy greater peace of mind?

- Today I will . . .

- This week I will . . .

- In the future I will . . .

NOTES

Chapter 1: What's Wrong with Me?

1. As cited in D. L. Moody, *Notes from My Bible and Thoughts from My Library* (Grand Rapids, MI: Baker Book House, 1979), p. 290.

2. Helen H. Lemmel, "Turn Your Eyes upon Jesus," 1922, first published in *Glad Songs* by the British National Sunday School Union.

3. Cited in Frank S. Mead, *12,000 Religious Quotations,* quoting Charles H. Mayo, *American Mercury* (Grand Rapids, MI: Baker Book House, 2000), p. 477.

Chapter 2: More Month Than Money

1. *USA Today,* January 12, 2009.

2. AP Press, 1/27/09, Washington, MSN home page.

3. William Hendriksen, *New Testament Commentary — Exposition of Philippians*

(Grand Rapids, MI: Baker Book House, 1975), p. 204.

4. Bruce B. Barton, *Life Application Bible Commentary — Matthew* (Wheaton, IL: Tyndale House Publications, 1996), p. 123.

Chapter 6: Why Do I Have to Be the Responsible One?

1. Bruce B. Barton, et al., *Life Application Bible Commentary — Luke* (Wheaton, IL: Tyndale House Publishers, Inc., 1997), p. 286.

Chapter 7: Be Careful with That!

1. Curtis Vaughan, gen. ed., *The Old Testament Books of Poetry from 26 Translations* — citing Kenneth N. Taylor (Grand Rapids, MI: Zondervan Bible Publishers, 1973), p. 189.

Chapter 8: I Don't Want to Go!

1. For the apostle Paul's understanding of this scene, read Romans 4:3–22 and Galatians 3:6–9.

Chapter 12: You Can Run, but You Can't Hide

1. Elvina M. Hall, "Jesus Paid It All," 1865.

2. Lila Empson, comp. and ed., *Words to Live by for Women* (Bloomington, MN: Bethany House, 2004), p. 88.

Personal Notes

Personal Notes

Personal Notes

Personal Notes

Personal Notes

Personal Notes

Personal Notes

Personal Notes

Personal Notes

ABOUT THE AUTHOR

Elizabeth George is a bestselling author who has more than 5 million books in print. She is a popular speaker at Christian women's events. Her passion is to teach the Bible in a way that changes women's lives.

For more information about Elizabeth's speaking ministry, to sign up for her mailings, or to purchase her books visit her website:

www.ElizabethGeorge.com

or call 1-800-542-4611

Elizabeth George
PO Box 2879
Belfair, WA 98528